TRAMWAY MEMOR
BELFAS

Desmond Coakham

Ian Allan
PUBLISHING

Contents

First published 2005

ISBN (10) 0 7110 3101 0
ISBN (13) 978 0 7110 3101 2

© Desmond Coakham 2005

Published by Ian Allan Publishing

an imprint of Ian Allan Publishing Ltd, Hersham, Surrey KT12 4RG.
Printed in England by Ian Allan Printing Ltd, Hersham, Surrey KT12 4RG.

Code: 0511/B

Visit the Ian Allan Publishing website at www.ianallanpublishing.com

Front: One of the 'McCreary' streamliners emerges from its secluded terminus at Ligoniel to commence the steep descent into Belfast — something line 1 in 10 here — down Ligoniel Road. The date is believed to be 6 June 1953.

Back: In Donegall Square North 'Chamberlain' No 376, in almost pristine condition, draws away from the 'tram island' that was as much the central point of Belfast tramways as Castle Junction itself. It has reached the destination shown on its indicators but will proceed along Wellington Place and reverse on the new crossover in College Square East. This was installed when the Balmoral route was abandoned in late 1952.

Title page: Balmoral car No 343 is running via Bedford Street on 11 September 1952 as it clears the Howard Street junction at the corner of Donegall Square West.

Introduction	3
Acknowledgements and References	4
Abbreviations Used in this Book	5
Historical Sketch	6
The Tramcar Fleet	14
Route by Route	28

Above: Displaying route 35 for Ligoniel, No 332 is at the end of the track on Donegall Road on 17 April 1947. Falls Road trolleybus route crosses in the background and Divis Mountain makes the skyline.

Introduction

Tramway memories? Urban dwellers of the writer's generation took electric trams for granted; we grew up with them and travelled to school on them, very often at a special 'juvenile' rate, visited relatives, were taken on them for Christmas shopping and summer excursions that included paddling, bathing and digging in the sand – provided you lived in a seaside town – or went on moorland rambles beyond the end of the tracks. Later there would be daily journeys to and from work in crowded tramcars and in all weathers; by then romance had faded and we were clad in wet raincoats, peering out of steamed-up windows. With the passage of time many of the trams had changed for the better: those with open-end balconies, to say nothing of completely open top decks, became rare and in the large towns totally enclosed double-deckers were commonplace. Around the year 1930 certain big cities went a step further and began to introduce a new standard of comfort and speed in their design, for they saw that the electric car had the advantage over omnibuses in dealing with mass transport in cities. Other places were seduced by attractive offers from major omnibus manufacturers and indeed 'changed horses in mid-stream' so that by the outbreak of World War 2 they were well on the way to ridding themselves of their tramways. The writer's home town was one such place and we seem to have accepted the superiority of rubber-tyred transport. The war changed all that. Imported petroleum became a precious commodity and most undertakings had to hang on to what remained of their electric tramways 'for the duration'. This was when I had a change of heart. A latent interest was revived, coincidentally, with a first reading of a novel, *The Good Companions*, by J. B. Priestley, a bluff Bradfordian with a remarkable gift for descriptive prose. It concerned a touring concert party whose bookings took them to towns up and down England of the 1920s, all with fictitious names of course. Nearly all of them had trams, and Priestley even told us what colour they were and added details like 'X was the place where the trams all turned around such-and-such a monument'. At that time I was familiar with no more than four tramways and one of these was very small indeed. So curiosity was aroused.

It was then that my work took me to Belfast. People who knew that city had told me about its introduction of trolleybuses. It was a pleasant surprise to find downtown Belfast swarming with trams, with hardly a trolleybus in sight, though the latter had the attraction of novelty. The liveries of blue and white and red and white added some cheer to the background of bombed sites left by the devastating air raids of the previous year. I never knew what Belfast's High Street was like before the blitz; a large part of its north side had been obliterated and the trams that traversed narrow Bridge Street now negotiated a vast wasteland. But the Albert Clock at the far end had survived, as has Sir Alfred Brumwell Thomas's City Hall that closed the vista looking south from Donegall Place. One had to get used to Donegal – with an extra 'l', all due to the clerk who mis-spelt the first Marquess's title on the documents of appointment. Neither were the Belfast Donegalls all in the one district, as we shall see.

My daily round had a lot to do with the requirements of the National Fire Service, into which the Belfast Fire Brigade had been gathered on the outbreak of war. An early assignment took me up the Crumlin Road, an eye-opener indeed, for as the tram climbed steadily westwards the landscape might well have been described by Priestley himself; street after street of brick-built terrace houses (but they were not back-to-back: they all had a nine-foot wide laneway behind their minuscule yards for the coalman and the binman. Much later, I would see my first genuine 'back-to-backs' from the upper deck of a Leeds tram; the penny dropped on seeing lines of washing across the side streets.) There were shops and pubs on the more important intersections, and every so often an enormous spinning mill. A variety of churches and chapels in every style of Victorian exuberance or austerity probably outnumbered the factories and mills. In the then-untroubled suburb of Ardoyne the double track from Shankill came in on our left. Soon there was another facing junction with double track swinging off right and ending at Ardoyne depot, magnificent in municipal brickwork, the last tram depot to be built in Belfast and made necessary by the need to shelter the extra trams to work the 1913

extensions. Straight ahead, Divis Mountain might well have been part of the Pennine chain, but Ligoniel was to be sampled another time. The last quarter-mile or so of that ascent was surely nearer 1 in 10 than the 1 in 15 quoted as Belfast's steepest gradient before the extensions had been made.

Ligoniel was one of the destinations to puzzle the stranger. There is equal emphasis on first and last syllable, but it can take some time to find this out. Likewise, 'M. Pottinger' might have been named after a Huguenot refugee, but the reader will see M stood for Mount. Castle Junction was always Castle Jn on the blinds. C.Down Ry stood for County Down Railway (the terminus in Station Street), while York Road station went from NCRY to LMS RLY NCC. The Great Northern terminus was represented only on 'via' blinds, but tautology was committed by the motor-buses when GNR Railway appeared. 'Donegall Pass' could mislead; that thoroughfare ran from Ormeau Road to Shaftesbury Square while a tram bearing the title was heading home from Sandy Row. Other towns had their depot-bound cars wind the blinds to blank and close the platform gates, but in Belfast it was usual to admit passengers on cars going out of service.

As the Belfast tramways had already been sentenced to death, it was not surprising to see that their permanent way had been allowed to deteriorate and in places flangeways had become shallow. One recalls the sight of the inner rail from Victoria Street to Chichester Street, a very tight curve close to the kerb outside Lavery's Bar, where the original groove had been widened by flange wear that formed two subsidiary grooves. It remained thus from long before 1942 to abandonment, yet a derailment there was never seen in many years of crossing that road; not necessarily to Lavery's, I hasten to add. But random relaying was already taking place and the Corporation was advertising for new rails and copper wire for the overhead. The Ministry of Supply seemed quite generous with the latter as the east Belfast routes were still being wired for conversion; remember that trolleybuses used twice as much overhead, indeed four times as much at junctions! An advertisement for 'special work' – the trade name for tailor-made points and crossings — obviously referred to the track fan at Salisbury Avenue depot that received a direct hit in the Blitz, and the plea must have been successful. There must also have been some recoverable material from abandoned routes. The outermost part of the Stormont line was less than 20 years old and it had been lifted from Stormont Gates to the 'Holywood Arches' (where it joined the Dundonald route) in a matter of weeks after trolleybus substitution, so perhaps not all the steel rails had been melted down for weapons of war. I can recall one length of new rail on the Ligoniel route where the road surface was renewed in concrete. The Glengormley line is recalled as being in reasonable shape, with fast running, notably by the 'Chamberlain' cars on evening trips from Bellevue. That line would have suited bogie cars admirably.

As for the tramcars themselves, the classes and their variants will be illustrated, but an observant man who served his apprenticeship at Sandy Row has asked the writer to nail a common misapprehension. The lighter colour of both tramcar liveries was never cream; it was always white enamel. Any cream effect came when the varnish began to discolour. Give the Transport Department its due, obsolete those cars might have been but the Belfast tram liveries were never allowed to reach the depths of neglect permitted by other UK transport

undertakings whose tram-scrapping programmes had been interrupted by the war. Repainting was carried out on a regular basis with some reduction in lining-out, and yellow paint replaced gold-leaf. Even the red cars that were first on the scrapping list when the trolleybuses began to multiply had their dashboards repainted in vermilion to cover the scars inflicted by the boots of homeward-bound shipyard workers. This was a phenomenon fortunately captured on camera when the wartime ban on photography was lifted, but we refer you to Mike Maybin's publications for some graphic images. At that time of day the writer was fighting his way against the tide of 'Islandmen' pouring down Station Street on foot and by tramcar.

This reckless behaviour, too widespread for anyone to prevent, had its occasional casualties. One incident related by a Tramways official concerned someone whose feet were crushed by the following car during an emergency stop. He had a chance of compensation as someone else had 'pushed a tram ticket into his hand'! The serious offence of smoking on the lower deck was tolerated on Queen's Road and in Station Street. Once, I boarded an inward-bound tram at the County Down station and the lower saloon was enveloped in a blue fog of tobacco smoke. I was told that on approaching Bridge End it was customary for the conductor to announce 'pipes out, gentlemen'. By that time I was on the upper deck where the

air was a lot clearer. This took place in mid-evening, well past the tea-time rush.

It is pleasant to know that one of the open-topped cars and a 'Chamberlain' are safely ensconced in the Ulster Folk and Transport Museum, but one feels regret that the unique type of top-covered 'standard red' had gone before the preservation movement gathered momentum. One of these would have been a fitting representative of the class that spent two world wars shifting the daily thousands on Queen's Road.

ACKNOWLEDGEMENTS AND REFERENCES

As a newcomer to the northern metropolis the writer was lucky in meeting like-minded people with a keen interest in their local tramways. Sadly but inevitably, those whose memories extended the furthest have all gone from us; they include Reg Ludgate, John H. McGuigan, Henry Rea, Cecil Slator and J. H. Smith. Of the succeeding generations, grateful thanks to Andrew Crockart, Davy Irwin, Jack Patience and Derek Young for help in various ways, and to visitors Richard Casserley, John Kennedy, Ian Yearsley and Terry Russell. A prime source of historical information was obtained from the issues of *Tramway and Railway World* mentioned in the following section, by courtesy of the National Tramway Museum at Crich, Derbyshire. The history of Belfast electric tramways serialised in *Tramway Review* by Mike Maybin, reprinted later in booklet

Opposite above: In Salisbury Avenue itself, No 368, which has probably replaced No 383 seen on page 30, is leaving the depot in the normal way, ie 'wrong road', and will turn left to join the outward track on Antrim Road.

Right: A motorised horse-car, No 232, is brought out for photography by the obliging depot staff at Knock on 6 May 1946.

form, is worth searching for by anyone eager for further detail, along with Mike's two other books, *A Nostalgic Look at Belfast Trams Since 1945* and his similarly titled *Belfast Trolleybuses* (Silver Link Publishing Ltd). J. Soper's seminal *History of Leeds Transport* has added some detail to Chamberlain's brief Managership in Belfast, while the *Belfast Street Directory* (Century Newspapers Ltd) has been a useful work of reference.

Picture Credits
All uncredited photographs are by the author.

ABBREVIATIONS USED IN THIS BOOK

BCT	Belfast City Tramways (later Transport)
BNCR	Belfast & Northern Counties Railway
BST	Belfast Street Tramways Co
GNR(I)	Great Northern Railway (Ireland)
LMS (NCC)	London, Midland & Scottish Railway (Northern Counties Committee) (successor to BNCR)
NIRTB	Northern Ireland Road Transport Board

Above: Glengormley terminus, with 'Chamberlain' No 348 awaiting departure, was still a County Antrim village when seen on 12 January 1949. Half a century later it has been engulfed in suburban growth and forms part of the district of Newtownabbey.

Historical Sketch

'An Extensive Electric System of the Latest Designs.' So ran the heading to the leading article in *Tramway and Railway World* for October 1905, describing the Belfast City Tramways that would be inaugurated on 29 November of that year. The articles did not lose sight of the fact that Belfast was the last major city in the United Kingdom to dispense with horse traction on its street tramways. One has to phrase this carefully, for Edinburgh, 'Athens of the North', was operating an extensive system of cable tramways and did not begin to electrify its routes until 20 June 1922, a task that was completed a year later. The neighbouring Burgh of Leith had already adopted electric traction, in the same year as Belfast, so that the inhabitants of Auld Reekie would by then have been familiar with this mode of transport and may well have seen its advantages.

Rails had first been laid in a Belfast street under an Act of Parliament of 1872, when the Belfast Street Tramways Company was formed. Prospects for the town as an industrial centre were already bright. The census for the previous year showed a population of 174,412 and this had passed the 350,000 mark by the time electric trams appeared on the scene. Its shipbuilding industry was embarking upon its greatest years, mill chimneys mushroomed as Irish linen products were sought after world-wide, there was a large ropeworks and many engineering establishments prospered as ancillaries to the basic industries . . . these were boom years indeed. After a shaky start, the horse tramways became well established and served a large part of the growing suburbs. Belfast received its charter as a City in 1892 and was a County Borough by 1898. Two years before that, the BST had secured powers for electrification. Perhaps the date, 1896, was significant, for Belfast's great rival, the capital city of Dublin, had opened its first electric tramway in that year. Caution was the watchword. Under the tramway legislation, company systems were under threat of municipalisation and their shareholders could come out of it badly. The BST, however, had an astute manager, Andrew Nance, who was extending the system with trackwork suitable for electric traction, and eventual legislation saw its undertaking purchased under the Belfast Corporation Act of 1904 for the sum of £356,948 14 shillings and 6 pence, to the satisfaction of all concerned. Unusually, Nance crossed the private/public divide and became the first General Manager of Belfast City Tramways, a post he held until 1916.

Once legal formalities were overcome, matters proceeded at a pace that should set an example to the 'footering'

Below: One end of the 'shed fan' in Gaffikin Street, looking towards 'the Row', 6 June 1953. The houses are occupied by Transport Department personnel and those toddlers have learned their road sense by now.

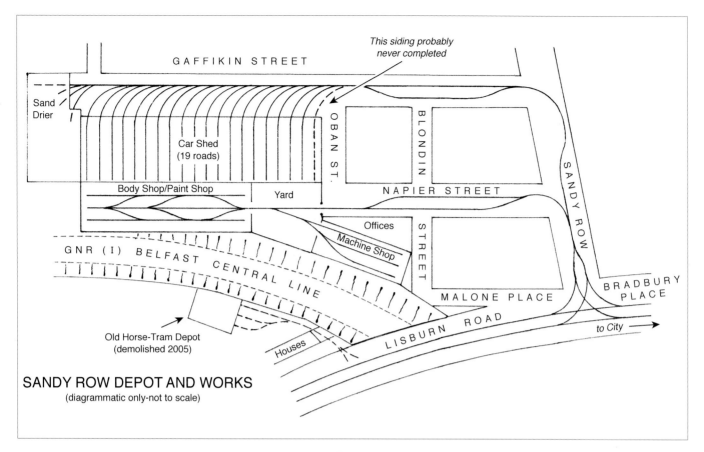

GAFFIKIN STREET

This siding probably never completed

Sand Drier

Car Shed (19 roads)

OBAN ST.

BLONDIN STREET

SANDY ROW

Body Shop/Paint Shop

Yard

NAPIER STREET

Offices

Machine Shop

STREET

GNR (I) BELFAST CENTRAL LINE

MALONE PLACE

BRADBURY PLACE

Old Horse-Tram Depot (demolished 2005)

Houses

LISBURN ROAD

to City

SANDY ROW DEPOT AND WORKS
(diagrammatic only-not to scale)

officialdom of the 21st century. There was a concerted effort by the relevant Corporation departments. In 1895, Belfast had begun generating its own electricity in a modest establishment at Chapel Lane, not far from the hub of the tramway system for which Nance had coined the title 'Castle Junction'. By 1898 demand had increased to the extent that a large coal-fired power station had been opened, having a capacity of 13,300 kilowatts. The City Electrical Engineer, Mr V. A. H. McCowan, was entrusted with both the necessary enlargement of this East Bridge Street plant and installation of the overhead equipment and general electrical work for the tramways. Mr H. A. Cutler, City Surveyor, collaborated in the extension of the power station building and was responsible for all the permanent way work. Contracts were placed with J. G. White & Co of London in the total sum of £543,404 for trackwork, overhead, underground feeder cables, engine — and boiler-house plant and 170 new electric tramcars, sub-contracted for as necessary. The Belfast firm of McLaughlin & Harvey, contractors with wide-ranging experience – they are still in business in 2005 — built the extended generating station for the contract sum of £19,690. Andrew Nance found himself with a free hand to convert existing depots for electrification and build new accommodation for the

increased stock of cars. This was all done by direct labour. The old BST workshops and car shed at Sandy Row required drastic rebuilding, and before the Brush Company at Loughborough could begin delivery of new cars, Nance needed a shed large enough to hold the expected 170 trams. This was sited on open ground behind the existing Falls Road horse-car depot at Andersontown that seems to have been the second of its kind of that route. The new building is stated to have had 12 roads (the final tram/trolleybus depot had 10) and was roofed with laminated timber principals, the famous 'Belfast' trusses that repeatedly appear in illustrations of Irish railway and tramway buildings. These were supported on 18in square pitch-pine pillars, a lavish operation by present-day standards, and the whole structure was clad with corrugated iron. The roof was finished with felt, another local product, and lavishly equipped with skylights.

When the *Tramway and Railway World* article was being written the Sandy Row alterations were far from complete. The 20-road car shed in Gaffikin Street was finished first. The magnificent 'shed fan' in manganese steel was manufactured by Hadfields Ltd of Sheffield and when re-assembled on site was within a 16th of an inch of its intended length. Photographs of the car shed include a couple of the

converted horse-cars, and here information becomes vague. We learn that the new body-shop had not been completed by opening day; its site was occupied by stabling for the tram horses, whose services would be required to the last hours before electrification. One can only guess that the horse-car conversions were carried out in the original workshop, presumably in a different part of the works. They do not appear in the official photographs of the temporary shed at Andersonstown. The Corporation had inherited a work-force skilled in coach-building from the old tram company that had been increasing its fleet and handed over 171 horse-trams at midnight on 31 December 1904.

The main contractors began work early in February 1905. There were the inevitable tales of disruption and inconvenience to the townsfolk, but the bulk of the system was operable by the end of that November, an amazing accomplishment in 10 months. The total route mileage of over $30\frac{1}{2}$ miles was mostly double track, with some interlaced track in Castle Street and Victoria Street, eventually doubled. Regarding overhead wiring, some wider streets in the city centre were given centre poles. Most routes used span wires between twin poles and at some places in the outer suburbs side poles with cantilever brackets were used;

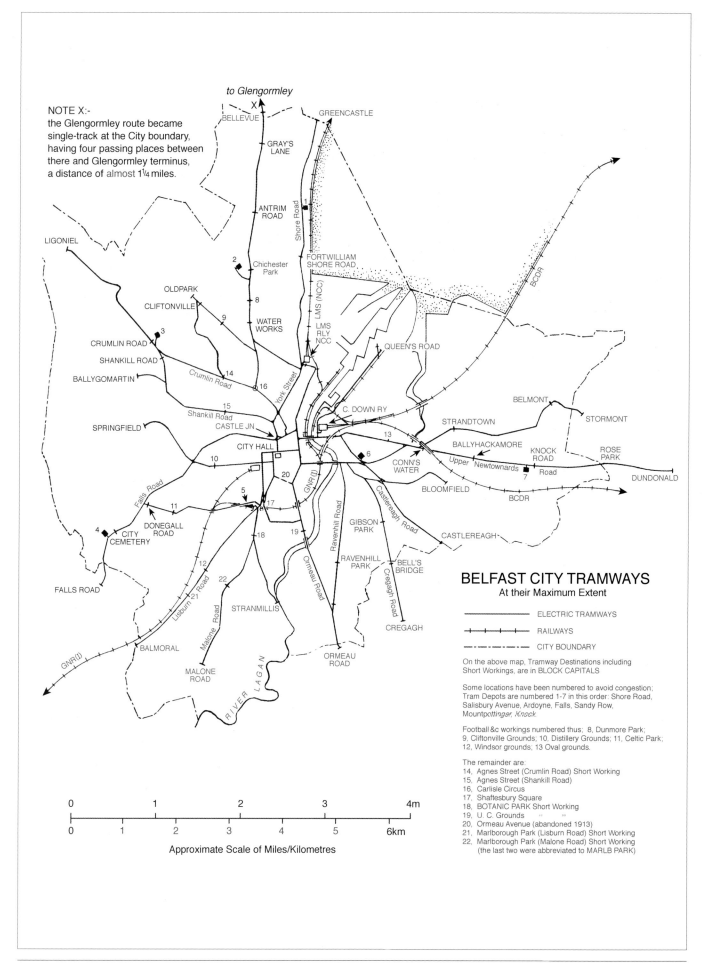

NOTE X:-
the Glengormley route became
single-track at the City boundary,
having four passing places between
there and Glengormley terminus,
a distance of almost 1¼ miles.

to Glengormley

X

BELLEVUE

GRAY'S
LANE

ANTRIM
ROAD

Chichester
Park

2

8

WATER
WORKS

Shore Road

1

FORTWILLIAM
SHORE ROAD

GREENCASTLE

X

BCDR

LIGONIEL

OLDPARK

CLIFTONVILLE

9

CRUMLIN ROAD
3

SHANKILL ROAD

BALLYGOMARTIN

Crumlin Road
14

16

LMS (NCC)

LMS
RLY
NCC

QUEEN'S ROAD

BELMONT

STORMONT

SPRINGFIELD

Shankill Road
15

CASTLE JN

CITY HALL

10

20

GNR(I)

C. DOWN RY

13

STRANDTOWN

BALLYHACKAMORE

KNOCK
ROAD

ROSE
PARK

Upper Newtownards Road

CONN'S
WATER

6

BLOOMFIELD

7

BCDR

DUNDONALD

CITY
CEMETERY
4

DONEGALL
ROAD

11

Falls Road

5

17

18

19

Ravenhill Road

GIBSON
PARK

Castlereagh Road

CASTLEREAGH

FALLS ROAD

12

21

Lisburn Road

22

STRANMILLIS

Malone Road

Ormeau Road

RAVENHILL
PARK

BELL'S
BRIDGE

Cregagh Road

CREGAGH

GNR(I)

BALMORAL

MALONE
ROAD

RIVER LAGAN

ORMEAU
ROAD

BELFAST CITY TRAMWAYS
At their Maximum Extent

———————— ELECTRIC TRAMWAYS

+—+—+—+—+ RAILWAYS

—·—·—·—·— CITY BOUNDARY

On the above map, Tramway Destinations including
Short Workings, are in BLOCK CAPITALS

Some locations have been numbered to avoid congestion;
Tram Depots are numbered 1-7 in this order: Shore Road,
Salisbury Avenue, Ardoyne, Falls, Sandy Row,
Mountpottinger, Knock.

Football &c workings numbered thus; 8, Dunmore Park;
9, Cliftonville Grounds; 10, Distillery Grounds; 11, Celtic Park;
12, Windsor grounds; 13 Oval grounds.

The remainder are:
14, Agnes Street (Crumlin Road) Short Working
15, Agnes Street (Shankill Road)
16, Carlisle Circus
17, Shaftesbury Square
18, BOTANIC PARK Short Working
19, U. C. Grounds   "   "
20, Ormeau Avenue (abandoned 1913)
21, Marlborough Park (Lisburn Road) Short Working
22, Marlborough Park (Malone Road) Short Working
   (the last two were abbreviated to MARLB PARK)

0   1   2   3   4m
0   1   2   3   4   5   6km
Approximate Scale of Miles/Kilometres

these had gone before the writer first traversed the system. As for centre poles, they seem never to have been popular in most cities (motorists hated them) and the Belfast examples were replaced by span wires at an early stage, with one important exception noted later. Belfast streets were paved with square setts from kerb to kerb for many years. Many tons of these were laboriously hand-made in the Ballygowan quarries 2 miles away in County Down and ended up as land-reclamation in Belfast Lough along with fragmented air-raid shelters. With a preponderance of horse traffic on the streets, the new electric trams were probably a lot quieter; it was customary also to use wood-block paving grouted with tar outside churches, hospitals and important buildings, and wood blocks were in turn hated by cyclists in wet weather. In low-lying central Belfast especially, built on sleech, subsidence caused tram rails and setts to part company here and there. As maintenance was neglected, trams became hated as well.

Ambiguities have surrounded the track gauge adopted by the two major Irish tramway systems, Dublin and Belfast. Both entered the horse-tramway era using the Irish railway gauge of 5ft 3in – or did they? In Belfast, cross-city connection between the three railway termini, Great Victoria Street (GNRI), York Road (BNCR) and Queen's Quay (BCDR/BHBR), stimulated the idea of a street tramway working between them that included conveyance of goods as well as passengers. In the capital there was physical connection between the urban horse tramways and the Dublin & Blessington Steam Tramway, all nominally 5ft 3in gauge. The latter company's rolling stock ran on railway profile wheels whose tyres were 5ft apart and 5in in width, incompatible with the grooved rail of street tramways to the same gauge. The solution was found by reducing the tramway gauge by approximately three-quarters of an inch, allowing tapering railway wheel flanges to run in the grooves of street tram track . . . this was overlooked by amateur historians for many years. Did Belfast tramways begin in the same way? It is now hardly relevant, for the BST obtained an Act in 1878 to convert its tracks to the British standard gauge of 4ft 8½in. The puzzle does not end there. Going forward several decades to 7 November 1947, the formerly progressive Liverpool City Tramways lost 66 trams, many of them modern, in a fire at its Green Lane depot. Offers of trams on loan came from more than one source. Blackpool's was turned down because that

system used a deeper flange profile and Belfast's offer refused even through Sandy Row offered to regauge surplus cars (no doubt 'standard reds') from 4ft 9in to Liverpool's 4ft 8½in. The Scouse capital found the Green Lane fire a means of hastening its tramway abandonment.

This caused a flurry of interest among our local aficionados but it was not pursued even though 'official' drawings gave the gauge as the British standard. Let us now quote again from *Tramway and Railway World*: 'The track has been laid to a gauge nominally 4ft 8½in but actually 4ft 9in.'

Came Opening Day, 29 November 1905, the first electric tram was driven by the Lord Mayor, Sir Daniel Dixon, a 'character' in his own right. Complaints about disruption were soon forgotten by the citizens who were clamouring for extensions, just as Dubliners have a century later with their second-generation system.

From 1905 until the outbreak of World War 1, Belfast tramways increased their mileage, firstly by completing the handful of authorised extensions remaining unbuilt. Most important of these was the Queen's Road route into the Harbour Estate on the east bank of the Lagan, where most of the shipbuilding activity was concentrated. The already-existing Station Street tramway was given a Y-junction with Bridge End and prolonged from its terminus in front of the BCDR station to the Harbour gates at the Abercorn Basin. From here the remaining mile of double track was the property of Belfast Harbour Commissioners, who had the overhead wiring carried on centre poles to be kept clear of the abnormal loads commonplace on Queen's Road in those prosperous days. The wide thoroughfare was also traversed by a rail track in heavy-section grooved rail with numerous sidings into engineering works, to say nothing of the multiple crossing leading from the coal quays at the Abercorn Basin. The Queen's Road tramway was inaugurated on 11 August 1908.

The fiefdom of the Belfast Harbour Commissioners covered the dock area on both sides of the river, Belfast Corporation having no jurisdiction over it. The Road Traffic Acts did not apply there; no licences were necessary for motor vehicles operating solely in the Harbour area, which was useful for the large engineering firms who had premises scattered over the estate. The Belfast Harbour Police were a separate body who also controlled gated 'frontier posts' at each road access, the terror of 'Islandmen' who were inclined to take home material they felt was in excess of shipbuilders' requirements. There were periodic scenes of panic at knocking-off

times when spot checks were carried out on the huge convoy of homeward-bound trams, occasions when many unclaimed objects were found at the roadside.

It is time to mention the Cavehill & Whitewell Tramway (C&WT), not a self-explanatory title, for we are looking at an extension (detached) of the BST's Antrim Road route which had gone no further than Chichester Park gates. Northwards to Glengormley village the Antrim Road rewarded travellers with picturesque glimpses of Belfast Lough and the rolling hills of County Down beyond. It became popular with the city's merchant princes, who established their estates and villas along the high ground. The C&WT received in 1881 an Order in Council under the Irish tramway legislation (Westminster was not involved) and was founded as a company with £6,000 capital. Unusually, it was to be steam-worked from the beginning and became the only street tramway in the area to operate bogie vehicles. Haulage was by conventional enclosed steam-tram locomotives from Messrs Kitson of Leeds. The engineer was John Lanyon, son of the famous Sir Charles. Under-capitalised to a niggardly extent for many years and modestly profitable, it opened on 1 July 1882, using the same gauge (4ft 9in) as BST. Nevertheless, a stubborn gap of a few yards that existed between the two systems at Chichester Park exemplified Belfast bloody-mindedness until acquisition by BCT, even through the enterprising Andrew Nance was a member of the C&W Board from 1892 and Chairman briefly in 1904, when he was obliged to resign on becoming Manager of the City Tramways.

Although its terminus was end-on to the city tramways, the C&WT was laid with grooved rail along the east side of the public road and was obliged to pave and maintain its right of way in the statutory manner. As the remainder of Antrim Road was waterbound macadam, other road traffic chose to use the better surface as well. Steam traction was given up after ten years, but two of the three tram-engines were kept for special workings for a while. The two bogie trailers would have gone with them. The length of route from Chichester Park to Glengormley is quoted as 3 miles 506yd, all single track with passing loops.

At the turn of the century the C&WT had attracted the attention of the British Electric Traction Company which was active in acquiring and electrifying street tramways all over the UK. An agreement was reached with BET and the requisite Act of Parliament obtained in 1902.

At this rate of progress it looked as if the C&W would leave Belfast City Tramways in second place for electric propulsion in the area but the next few years were occupied in obscure negotiation that needs someone to unravel. A contract was placed with the builders of the city tramways, J. G. White & Co, and the electric tramway to Glengormley opened for business on 17 February 1906. A new single line was laid in the middle of the road and more generously provided with passing places than the horse tramway, which incidentally was able to function while the electric line was being built. An electric car shed was built at the (new) Bellevue gardens on the city boundary, the Glengormley steam/horse depot being disposed of. The original Bellevue Pleasure Gardens nearby were retained by BCT when the C&WT was purchased from BET in 1911, until the second Bellevue was ready for pleasurable purposes. So the silly 35yd gap at Chichester Park was at last closed, and BCT wasted no time in doubling the Antrim Road line as far as it was allowed.

A further spate of tracklaying in 1913 brought the route mileage up to 49. There were now 18 outer termini with a web of tramways linking them to Castle Junction.

Proceeding clockwise from Falls Road in the south-west and climbing the high ground where mill chimneys began to proliferate between the ranks of terrace houses, Springfield terminus came next, then Ligoniel. The extended Ligoniel route had reached the mill village itself by then; the Oldpark Road route and Cliftonville were within yards of each other and joined, perhaps for some forgotten idea of extension. Glengormley was at the north point of our irregular circuit, then Greencastle on the Lough shore, Queen's Road in the massive shipbuilding complex on the east bank of the Lagan, Belmont in a greener suburb close to the Holywood hills, with the Newtownards Road almost due east reaching the city boundary at Knock — it would cross to the outskirts of Dundonald by 1924. Bloomfield was at the end of a short line, close to Ballyhackamore on the Newtownards Road and seemed to have a cosier atmosphere than most termini; North Road didn't lead to anywhere in particular at that time. Castlereagh Road, leading to the Hill Foot Road in the south-east, was in a developing residential area, as was Cregagh, while due south, the Ormeau Road route didn't quite reach Newtownbreda. Back on the west bank of

the Lagan, Stranmillis had a secluded air and the route might have been busier if Andrew Nance's notion of prolonging it to Shaw's Bridge (a weekend resort) had been accepted by the Council. The Malone Road terminus was something of an anticlimax and the rails should have gone further; linked to it by several avenues of good-quality housing was Balmoral on the busy Lisburn Road, the 18th terminus, close to the GNR main line and looking across the Bog Meadows to Falls Road where this survey began.

There were other, shorter, routes linking the trunk lines; from the multiple junction at Shaftesbury Square the Donegall Road route connected at its terminus with the Falls Road line and there may have been through workings to the City Cemetery which was a wholly Protestant enclave (albeit quieter than some) as the Catholic Church did not wish to share such municipal facilities. At the time (1913) of

Below: A covey of three 'Moffetts' have gathered at the Ormeau terminus on 6 April 1948, the nearest being No 333. Tracks ended at the Galwally Park road junction, out of sight on the right. The spire of Newtownbreda Presbyterian Church is a prominent landmark.

such tramway activities, the first abandonment took place when Ormeau Avenue ceased to be an alternative route for Ormeau Road and was replaced by a line from Shaftesbury Square by Botanic Avenue that threaded the inner city residential area around the University and rejoined Ormeau Road shortly before it crossed the Lagan. On the east side of that river was the unluckiest of Belfast's tram routes, the Ravenhill Road line. It ran southwards from the Albert Bridge crossing, firstly through a small industrial area of east Belfast, where the Albert Boiler Works and Scott's Volt Works, electrical manufacturers, were probably the best examples of heavy industry. The line's first outer terminus was at South Parade, but in 1913 the route was extended to a double junction with the Ormeau Road line. Yet later that same year, Nance was proposing to cut the service back to its original terminus. Its lack of appeal seems to have been due to the small catchment area; this tapered to a point on the west side as it approached Ormeau Road. A large part of the Ravenhill Road frontage was taken up by the Marquess of Donegall's gift to the City, the Ormeau Park, and most visitors to that place of recreation probably found it more convenient to reach the Park on

the Ormeau Road trams. The route did have a sporting venue to boost its takings. A couple of blocks short of South Parade was Ravenhill Park, home of the Irish Rugby Football Union's Ulster branch and this shared international Rugby matches with Lansdown Road in Dublin until a few years after World War 2. Here, however, the motor-bus abstracted most of the extra revenue, for patrons were taken right into the ground. This recalls an amusing problem for the Transport Department. There is or was, a sort of triumphal arch at the entrance, and a double-decker in the queue under this arch found itself trapped when its passengers left en masse, causing the bus to rise on its springs. The enterprising crew freed it by letting the tyres down. One up for buses, we suppose. Nowadays the most exciting event at Ravenhill is probably the Schools Cup on St Patrick's Day.

Two further tramway extensions, to Ballygomartin (the nineteenth terminus) from Woodvale on the Shankill and to Stormont from the old Belmont terminus, completed the Belfast tramway system and are illustrated in the 'Route by Route' section. These had been planned during the brief regime of Nance's successor, J. S. D. Moffett. He began well, drawing

attention to the need for track renewal over a large part of the system. This was always a weak point in first-generation electric tramways, initially profitable to the extent that these profits were siphoned off for the relief of rates. Moffett's relaying scheme, not complete until June 1926, cost nearly a million-and-a-quarter pounds sterling; by then he was comfortably settled as general manager of Salford City Tramways. The lesson was never learned by Belfast Corporation.

In that brave new post-war world of the early 'twenties, James Moffett roused his transport committee to face the possibility, if not the necessity, of tramway extensions. His concern centred around the congestion caused by the large peak hour traffic patterns not only on Queen's Road itself, where he envisaged alternative access, but also in central Belfast, where Nance's 'all cars pass the Junction' policy had been self-defeating. Moffett's most useful contribution was revival of the long-forgotten intention of a tramway along Chichester Street between Donegall

Below: Autumn sunshine on Scots pines, neat domestic housing and No 419 looking clean and quite modern . . . Ballygomartin has a homely air about it on 24 October 1952.

Square and Victoria Street, carried out in 1924. Perhaps we have a date for the well-worn curve at Lavery's corner. Other curves laid down to carry shipyard traffic clear of the city centre were between North Street and Royal Avenue and Royal Avenue, and Donegall Street (for Shankill Road cars) and from Brougham Street into York Street and from Whitla Street likewise, though in the opposite direction. Cars from Queen's Road might now reach the Antrim Road and avoid the city centre, in conjunction with the new single track in front of the Albert Clock. This required a facing crossover in Victoria Street south of the new triangular layout if it was to function in both directions but we have yet to see an Ordnance map showing such a feature. A matter of yards further south, at the Ann Street-Victoria Street 'delta', was the last surviving facing crossover that will be seen in operation for the benefit of a UC Grounds-Queen's Road car later on in these pages. The writer would be glad to learn of other such examples in these islands; the Infirmary Junction in Cardiff is the only one that comes to mind. The London Metropolitan Police, with its own nanny state for wheeled vehicles, would have hardly countenanced the practice of wrong-line running around corners.

After Moffett's departure the history of Belfast Tramways ran a parallel course with many other undertakings of similar magnitude. There was the 1920s 'bus war'

when private enterprise of all shapes and sizes found the trams to be fair game for omnibus competition. A previously well-run municipal system came under severe financial pressure. The new General Manager, Samuel Carlisle, had come up through the Tramways Department and whatever his merits, proved the adage about a prophet being without honour in his own country, for he had his enemies on the Tramways Committee and became the scapegoat for all ills suffered by his department. Perhaps we might have had a 'Carlisle' tramcar, for there was still strong feeling that the tram was a necessary people-shifter in large cities. Fare increases did little for public opinion, and Maybin has aptly pointed out that Belfast Corporation brought the bus war on its own head by failing to read the small print of Stormont legislation on the subject; it did not revise its own byelaws while the chance was there.

While Carlisle was superseded as general manager in 1928 (he had incidentally introduced the first Corporation omnibus services) he remained in a senior post and was acting General Manager when Chamberlain left at short notice in 1931 until Robert McCreary was confirmed as the new occupant. Not only that; when McCreary was recalled to military service on the outbreak of World War 2, Carlisle was once more in his old post, and he was an

honoured guest on Belfast's last tramcar on 27 February 1954.

The seeds of tramway abandonment were sown when Belfast obtained powers in 1930 to operate trolleybuses. The first route to be converted was Falls Road on 28 March 1938. The big six-wheelers were a great success with the public. Conversion was in full swing when war broke out. It had been scheduled for completion by 1944, this being obviously delayed by war conditions, but enough material was in hand and sufficient vehicles obtained to convert the Cregagh, Castlereagh, Stormont and Dundonald routes by the end of 1943. Meanwhile, the trams that remained came into their own as never before, surviving a severe baptism of fire in the air raids of spring 1941. Much disruption was caused but only Salisbury Avenue depot received a direct hit. Two red cars were written off.

However, the 'finest hour' of Belfast tramways was at hand. Despite having lost several important routes to trolleybuses, the tramways were carrying record numbers of passengers. Nett profit of the combined undertaking for 1941/2 had been £72,358. The trams had earned a nett surplus of £40,549 and their working profit had been £140,049. £10,000 was available for rate relief. In the last 12 months of hostilities profits were: motor-buses £82, trolleybuses £58,292 and trams £69,285. There were some hard winters in that

Above: **Whitla Street on 14 January 1949. The truncated remains of York Road station and hotel form a depressing backcloth to No 357 on Route 25 this winter's day.**

Above: **Three 'McCrearys', a bus and lots of pedestrians in Donegall Place on 16 October 1952. No 394 is heading for Springfield. The writer has grumbled about trolleybus overhead elsewhere but admits that what is seen here makes for an interesting composition.**

wartime period. An example was the blizzard of 5/6 March 1942 when the Transport Department rose to the occasion, running an all-night snow-plough operation, backed up by a continuous 'service' on all tram routes. It was said that these trams ran two abreast along the streets, but the crews must have had a difficult time watching for trailing crossovers, usually half a mile apart. And there was a black-out as well as a white-out.

In the 'peace' that followed in 1945, Europe had Marshall-aid by the bucketful while the UK endured shortages of nearly everything. Hence the snail's-pace of tramway conversion in Belfast; trolleybuses began to make a half-hearted come-back but the last direct conversion of a tram route to trolleybus was Greencastle in 1950.

Trams had a habit of 'helping out' on routes that were officially closed to them. Lisburn Road was a case in point, a rush-hour 'Windsor Grounds' working soon became an all-day service. Sunday visitors to the City Hospital (Lisburn Road) and Royal Victoria at the top of Grosvenor Road had tram services too, the latter on the otherwise abandoned Springfield route. These petered out in mid-1953. The

Ligoniel route was the last survivor, retaining a service on both Shankill and Crumlin roads, with some cars continuing to the Queen's Quay Station tram siding until Saturday 30 October 1953. Ardoyne depot continued to provide the workmen's trams to and from Queen's Road until Friday 12 February 1954. Mountpottinger depot had closed on the fourth of that month. By then the tramcar fleet had shrunk to 41 cars, all 'Chamberlains' except 'rebuild' No 288. The official 'Funeral' procession of 12 'Chamberlains', the first 11 of which were available to the public at six old pence a head, left Queen's Road for Ardoyne depot on Saturday 27 February.

While the Transport Department is stated to have lost money after 1947, press reports in those last years indicate that the trams were making a trading profit almost up to the end.

The picture is not really complete without rounding off the history of electricity generation in Belfast. From the early years of East Bridge Street power station the demand for electricity saw continuous growth. By 1923 the former was on standby, superseded by a new Harbour power station, the latter augmented in 1955

by the West Power Station across the Lagan. Both fed also into the Northern Ireland grid. Municipal electrical generation was traditionally coal-fired and it cost the citizens a good deal less than that produced for the rest of the Province by the Electricity Board for Northern Ireland in its largely oil-fired stations. How this situation was tolerated during the dollar-hungry years that followed World War 2 is not clear. Belfast resisted surrendering its generating capacity until the upheaval of Edward Heath's local government reorganisation in 1973. By then Belfast Corporation has lost control of its motor-buses, and its profitable coal-gas plant had been persuaded to change to 'cheap' oil-gas that would be otherwise burnt off as waste by a new oil refinery on the Harbour Estate. Where is that now? The obvious advantage of trolleybus operation was the continuous use of indigenous coal. Even that went sour in 1959 when the Transport Committee recommended their replacement by motor-buses. The trolleys had gone by 12 May 1968. By then, with the resurfacing of Belfast streets with asphalt in place of ill-maintained square setts, the trolleybuses' appalling vibration had been greatly moderated . . . but let us look at some more trams.

The Tramcar Fleet

THE RED CARS: RINGING THE CHANGES

Belfast's municipal Transport Department always adopted a single numbering system for each of the three forms of passenger vehicle it operated — trams, motor-omnibuses and trolleybuses were each numbered in a separate list from 1, and as individual vehicles were withdrawn, replacements or additions to stock received new numbers at the end of the list. But we shall encounter one inexplicable exception to the rule.

The first electric tram cars, built at the Brush Company's Loughborough factory and numbered 1-170 were conventional single-trucked open-topped double-deckers. They were unvestibuled (ie without glazing to the end platforms) but canopied so that the full length of the top deck was available for seating. During the horse-car era customers had become used to exposure on the open top decks, but at the late date of 1905 more progressive cities in the UK had been developing top covers, usually with end balconies, and in a couple of years Belfast followed suit, rebuilding the first 170 to its own distinctive style so that only a few very early photographs of the original cars in their open-top mode have survived. Dimensions were: length overall 28ft,

width 6ft 10in; three-window bodies 16ft over pillars, seating 22 on longitudinal slatted wood seats in the lower saloon and 32 passengers on tip-over garden seats above. They were carried on Brush-Brill 21E trucks having a 6ft 6in wheelbase. Braking was manual with rheostatic back-up. The writer was delighted to see that these red cars had the pudding-basin-shaped brass wheels surrounding the conventional handbrake pillars, the former operating the slipper brakes that gripped each railhead, last seen by him on the trams of Newport, a town that closed its system in 1937 and had gradients like those in west Belfast. Each car was powered by two Westinghouse 35hp motors.

While Brush was delivering the 170 'Standard Reds' to the temporary assembly shop at Falls horse-car depot, the Tramways Department had selected 50 of its best horse-cars (build by the Belfast Street Tramways at Sandy Row) for conversion to electric traction, allocating them the numbers 201-250. Early photographs show them to have had completely open platforms without canopies. They were noticeably shorter than the Brush cars, their three-window bodies (14ft over pillars and seating 20) perched on 5ft 6in trucks. When

canopied the upper deck held 28. Top-covering began more or less simultaneously with the Brush cars and to the same style, the upper saloons having a central window and a half-size window each side. The conversions were easily recognisable, with a markedly deeper rocker panel above the rubbing-strake and vertically slotted ventilators above the top-lights in the lower saloon, caused by the old-fashioned monitor roof (an American feature) from the horse-cars. The last seven of the series (244-250) remained open-topped to the end but were given canopied platforms like the original electric cars. They appeared regularly in fine summer weather, especially on workings to Bellevue. No 245 was decorated and illuminated for special occasions. World War 2 put paid to this activity and she was last seen in a ruinous conditions at Knock depot in 1945, no doubt raided for spare parts. Some of these seven, including No 249, now happily in the Ulster Folk and Transport Museum, have caused speculation among historians as to whether they were truly ex-horse — they lack the monitor roofs — but there are memories of a depot fire that necessitated new ceilings and consequent replacement of lower-saloon ventilators to the

Right: 'Standard Red' No 194, putative rebuild of a Cavehill & Whitewell Company's tramcar, was the only car of its type to receive a complete repaint after World War 2; indeed none are thought to have been so treated since 1939. Only the lining has been simplified, as became standard practice with the 'Blue Cars'. No 194 stands proudly in Gaffikin Street, Sandy Row, on 8 November 1945.

Opposite: Drawing of a 'standard' car.

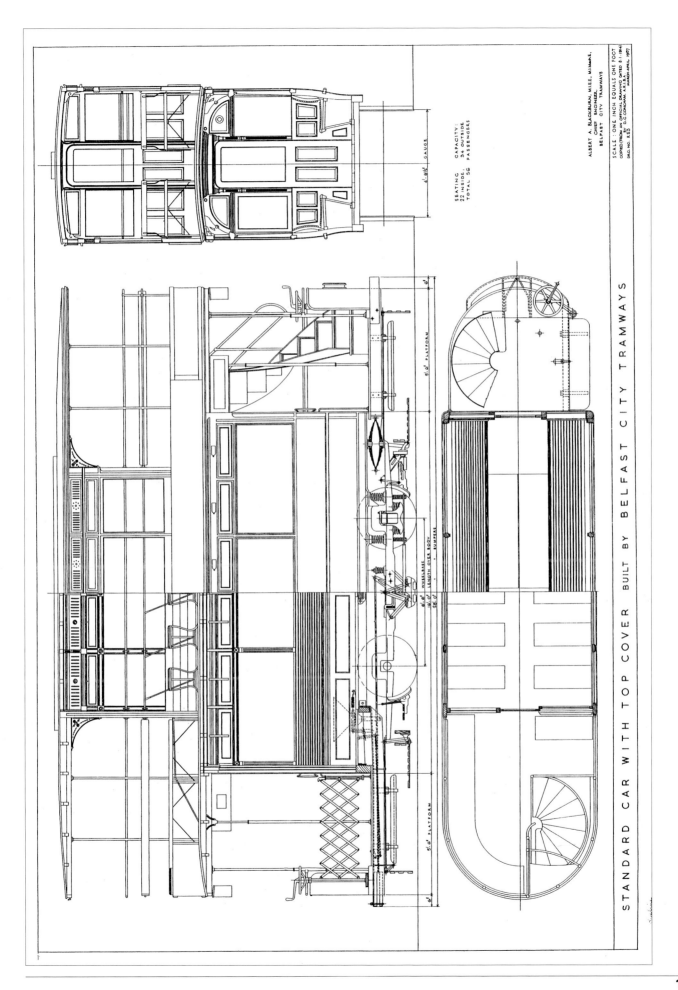

STANDARD CAR WITH TOP COVER BUILT BY BELFAST CITY TRAMWAYS

SEATING CAPACITY:
22 INSIDE. 34 OUTSIDE.
TOTAL 56 PASSENGERS

ALBERT A. BLACKBURN, M.I.E.E., M.I.Mech.E.,
CHIEF ENGINEER,
BELFAST CITY TRAMWAYS

SCALE: ONE INCH EQUALS ONE FOOT
COPIED FROM AN OFFICIAL DRAWING DATED 8.11.1914
BY D.G. COAKHAM, A.R.I.B.A. MARCH-APRIL 1957
DWG. NO. X&D

standard design. Compare the illustrations in this section.

With the 50 motorised horse-cars on the streets, Sandy Row body shop soon filled up again as production of home-built standard cars — now with top covers — commenced in earnest. Further examples of the 'long-top saloon' variant appeared among the 171-192 batch (1908-1910) but the 251-291 series (1913-on) reverted to the earlier design. Was the forceful manager, Andrew Nance, responsible for its perpetuation? He was a great believer in fresh air, at least for his motormen, whom he denied vestibuled platforms. Nothing definite may be written about the red cars that carried numbers 193-200 and are regarded as rebuilds from the eight cars taken over in 1911 from the electrified Cavehill & Whitewell Tramway. Three of these were long-bodied double-decks on radial trucks, and 'rebuilding' in this case may have been a book-keeping convenience.

Right: Seen in Knock depot yard on a November day in 1946, No 80 was one of the few 'Standards' given a long-wheelbase (7ft 6in) truck at an unknown date.

Below: Work-worn No 18, broadside-on at Mountpottinger depot, has been top-covered with a full-length saloon but retains its 6ft 6in Brush-Brill truck, 4 September 1945.

Right: 'Long top saloon' No 173 rests along with a contemporary road vehicle at Bloomfield terminus on 27 March 1946. No 173 has been given a 7ft 6in wheelbase truck with sturdier half-elliptical springs.

Below right: 'Odd man out' since her upper-deck enclosure in 1923, the solitary No 89 ploughs a lonely furrow (or two?) through the coal dust of Queen's Quay Road on 8 March 1946. Most of the Belfast coal importers were established at the 'coal quay' here. Their cranes are busy in the background; it is an activity that has vanished entirely.

Above: We can show you five of the seven open-top former horse cars. No 244 was one that got away, but we know she had the platform grilles and the horsecar ceiling. The illuminated No 245 had gone before we knew what we were looking for, but here is No 246 at Knock depot on 6 May 1946, minus snowplough and life-guard, but the top-lights in the saloon have slotted vents above them to show the ceiling has the same profile as those carried by the top-covered conversions. Also note the three quarter-elliptical springs.

Left: No 213 and her ilk had been in great demand for snowplough duties in the horrendous winter of 1947. Still carrying her ploughs, she is seen in retirement at Knock depot on 9 May of the same year. Note the straightness of her bodywork after decades of successive horse and electric traction.

Below: We don't know how many of the converted horse-cars retained the decorative wrought-ironwork on their platforms when rebuilt, but a handful of them survived into post-war days. Here is No 223 at Knock depot on 6 May 1946. They looked nice, but were they draughty for the motormen?

Left: On 4 September 1945, No 247 is still in passenger service and will shortly leave Knock depot for Queen's Road. The arrangement of ventilators above top-lights shows the ceiling to have been reconstructed. The truck has full elliptical springs.

Below: The most interesting conversion was that of No 248, equipped as a rail-grinder; note the wooden water-barrel on the top deck and the snug vestibuling on each platform. Again, upperworks show evidence of renewal and springs are full-elliptical. There is a large red light above the driver's window. Rail-grinding was a night-time operation. The date is 4 September 1945.

Right: Seen on the Gaffikin Street shed-fan, No 249 ended its career as snowplough and general dogsbody at Sandy Row. It also has had a roof and ceiling replacement. We can still savour it at the Ulster Folk and Transport Museum, carrying a waxwork tableau of Belfast life on the top deck. The date is 6 June 1953.

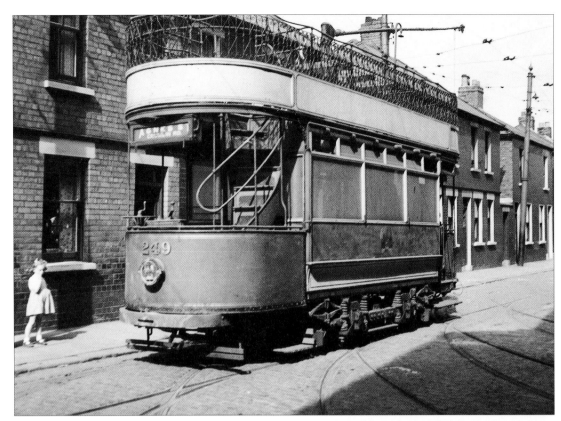

Below: The last open-topper, No 250 was photographed at Mountpottinger depot on 4 September 1945. Four reconstruction jobs have been accounted for, including that of No 250. The very old destination blind 'NCRY' (Northern Counties Railway) would have been a trophy worth having.

THE 'MOFFETTS'

J. S. D. Moffett, who came from West Ham Corporation Tramways in 1916, moved the Belfast system a notch or two further into the 20th century by ordering 50 more cars from the Brush Company when materials became available after World War 1. Here were Belfast's first totally enclosed tramcars, once again on Brill single trucks but with a wheelbase of 7ft 6in and powered by 40hp motors. They seated 26 in the lower and 42 in the upper saloon. Their original front-exit arrangement was a good idea but probably too advanced for conservative Belfast, for it

was soon removed. The totally enclosed cars must have looked smart in the vermilion and white livery. Moffett would have submitted a specification to Brush, but what involvement he had in detail design is unknown. The 'Moffetts' were externally similar to cars other undertakings put on the road in the 1920s; the four upper saloon windows each side opened and closed simultaneously through gearing operated by the conductor. The new cars were delivered between late 1920 and mid-1921. Principal dimensions were: length overall 30ft 10in, outside width 6ft 9in

(lower saloon) and 7ft 1in (upper saloon). Hardwood seating on both decks was still the norm for tramcars in large industrial towns, but the accession of William Chamberlain to the Belfast managership in 1929 was welcomed most of all by tramcar patrons when stuffed leather seating appeared in the 'Moffetts'. They may not have noticed the mechanical improvements that accompanied the upholstery. The class was re-trucked with Maley & Taunton 8ft wheelbase swing-link trucks with 50hp motors. And it was given Chamberlain's dark blue and white livery.

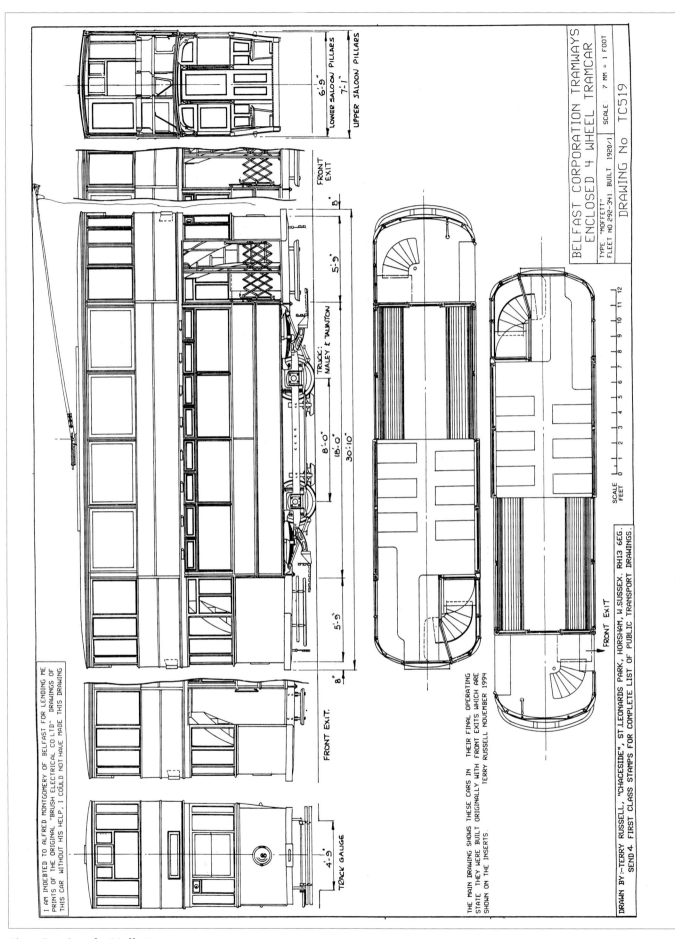

The drawing contains the following labels and text:

BELFAST CORPORATION TRAMWAYS ENCLOSED 4 WHEEL TRAMCAR

TYPE "MOFFETT"
FLEET NO 292–341 BUILT 1920/1 SCALE 7 MM = 1 FOOT

DRAWING No TC519

LOWER SALOON PILLARS 6'-9"
UPPER SALOON PILLARS 7'-1"

FRONT EXIT

8"

5'-9"

TRUCK: MALEY & TAUNTON

8'-0"
18'-0"
30'-10"

5'-9"

8"

FRONT EXIT.

4'-9"
TRACK GAUGE

SCALE FEET 0 1 2 3 4 5 6 7 8 9 10 11 12

FRONT EXIT

I AM INDEBTED TO ALFRED MONTGOMERY OF BELFAST FOR LENDING ME PRINTS OF THE ORIGINAL "BRUSH ELECTRICAL CO LTD" DRAWINGS OF THIS CAR WITHOUT HIS HELP, I COULD NOT HAVE MADE THIS DRAWING

THE MAIN DRAWING SHOWS THESE CARS IN THEIR FINAL OPERATING STATE THEY WERE BUILT ORIGINALLY WITH FRONT EXITS WHICH ARE SHOWN ON THE INSERTS.   TERRY RUSSELL NOVEMBER 1994

DRAWN BY:-TERRY RUSSELL, "CHACESIDE", ST LEONARDS PARK, HORSHAM, W.SUSSEX. RH13 6EG. SEND 4– FIRST CLASS STAMPS FOR COMPLETE LIST OF PUBLIC TRANSPORT DRAWINGS.

Above: Drawing of a 'Moffett' car.

REBUILDING THE RED CARS

Availability of 50 surplus 7ft 6in trucks gave new life to a similar number of the old unvestibuled double-deckers. Rebuilding to totally enclosed form began with No 164 in early 1929. The last 41 of the Belfast-built 'Reds', Nos 251-291 and eight other older cars, Nos 21, 22, 31, 35, 78, 123, 159 and 186, were converted at Sandy Row and by outside contractors, the Service Motor Works of east Belfast. In general, the deep upper saloon windows were retained while sills at vestibuled ends were raised to conform to later practice. This made their origin very obvious but a few cars came out with top-deck sills of uniform height. Perhaps this added to the cost. Mr Chamberlain's blue livery first appeared on the rebuilds. It was given also to a few unvestibuled cars — Nos 57, 124 and 146 have been recorded. They were soon repainted red and white when it was decided that only upholstered cars would be blue.

Right: At Donegall Road terminus on 17 April 1947, No 284 illustrates the majority of Chamberlain's rebuilt 'Standard' cars.

Above: Included to show the rare alternative of level window sills on the upper deck, rebuilt No 78 stands in Mountpottinger depot yard on 6 June 1953. To express a personal opinion, the writer feels that this treatment gave the rebuilds a more business-like appearance.

THE 'CHAMBERLAINS'

Mr Chamberlain (later Sir William) had a short but turbulent career as Tramways Manager in Belfast, quickly going on to higher things as Chairman of Traffic Commissioners for the North West Area (GB), where he earned his knighthood in 1939. He died at the early age of 67 in 1944. As General Manager of Leeds City Tramways from 1925, he made his name in that tram-orientated place by introducing a totally-enclosed four-wheel double-decker, painted in what was called 'Princess Blue' livery. Local tram fans gave this design the 'Chamberlain' appellation and also bestowed the name 'Horsfield' on the cars produced by his successor. As the naming of tramcar types after the manager in post was at least semi-official in Belfast it may well be that the practice was copied by north of England aficionados. The 50 trams (342-391) that were built by Brush of Loughborough were superficially similar to the Leeds cars, but it is interesting to see that Chamberlain's first cars were a follow-on from Leeds' totally enclosed design dating from 1923. These had four-window bodies 17ft long on Peckham 'P22' 7ft 6in wheelbase trucks and were 29ft 6in over platforms, with seating for 70. Chamberlain had built an experimental car with the same body in 1925. It included several features he had used in Oldham. The upper deck was unobstructed through its length, unhampered by the bulkheads that traditionalists had perpetuated from the 'balcony' era. This car had an EMB 'pivotal' truck that was occupying the attention of Leeds Tramways Committee. The standard Leeds 'Chamberlain' (185 were built) had an 18ft body, was 31ft long overall and seated 26 on longitudinal seats downstairs and 46 (2 and 2) above. The 10ft wheelbase pivotal (radial) trucks gave endless trouble, but Chamberlain cannot be blamed.

Belfast's 'Chamberlains' chuntered happily along on 8ft Maley & Taunton trucks and were 19ft long over body; platforms were shorter at 5ft 9in and length over bumpers was 31ft 10in. Seats for 24 in the lower saloon were arranged with four rows of 'two and one' transverse seats and four three-seater longitudinal in the corners. In the upper saloon were eight rows of '2 and 2' seating and a further six seats at each stairhead, a grand total of 68. The Belfast cars scored for comfort; Leeds had to make do with wooden seats on both decks until cushioning came in the 1930s and the '2 and 1' arrangement was adopted in the lower saloon.

Below: By 1952, Belfast City Transport was able to set a date for final abandonment of its trams. Unlike some once great systems, which sickened their clients by letting their cars deteriorate to a shocking state, civic pride asserted itself and a quantity of 'Chamberlain' cars was selected for final repainting. At the end in February 1954 none was in a really shabby state. This is No 354 at Springfield terminus on 15 October 1952, not long out of the paint shop.

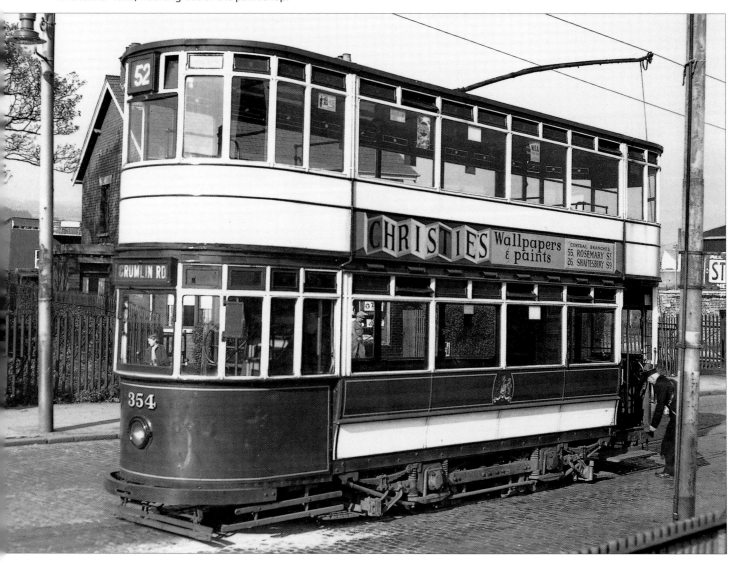

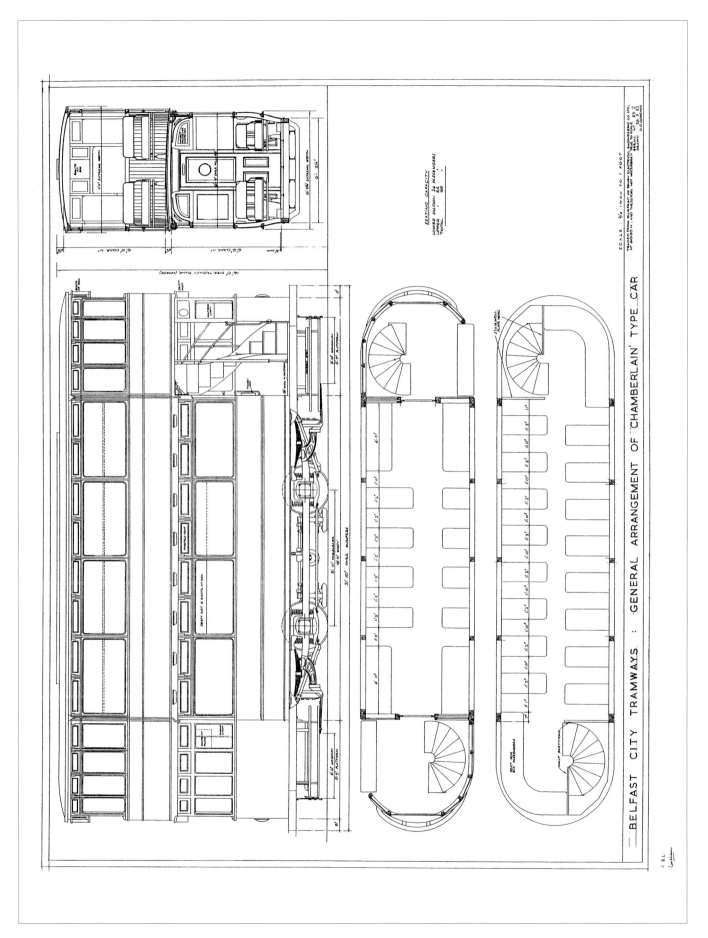

Above: Drawing of a 'Chamberlain' car.

THE 'McCREARYS'

Beauty may be in the eye of the beholder, but more than one person who recalls the last 50 trams built for Belfast will claim that they were among the best-looking of their kind built in the British Isles in the 1930s, the decade that saw the limited emergence of the 'modern tramcar'. Looking at their photographs today, one finds them hard to describe as 'dated' apart from the old-fashioned lining and the four-wheeled truck. Imagine a 'McCreary' on eight wheels!

Perhaps we were lucky to have them. The Corporation had powers for operating trolleybuses and planning for the first route must have commenced already. It has been said that these cars were designed for a short life — hence the weakness encountered with platform bearers, exacerbated by wartime overloading on the Queen's Road route. This was not an altogether convincing explanation, as the trouble manifested

itself when the first cars were delivered in 1935. Mr J. M. Maybin has established that the McCreary design originated in 1934 with the English Electric Company of Preston, which was responsible for building 19 of the 50 cars, including the prototype No 392 that along with 393 was given a separate driver's compartment. In the writer's tram-riding days this pair were very rare birds indeed. Fortunately, the emergence of drawings by the Service Motor Works of Belfast has allowed Mr Terry Russell of Horsham to produce plans, elevations and a section (reproduced herein with grateful thanks) that include the cab arrangements of Nos 392 and 393. One suspects that the restricted entrance/exit for passengers led to modification of the remaining 48 cars, 31 of which including No 393 were built, or rather assembled, by the Service Motor Works who had already enclosed Chamberlain's 'rebuilds'. Body components or, at the least, jigs would

have come from English Electric. It has been noticed that differences between the two batches of cars have been mainly in internal finishes and headlight positions. The 'McCrearys' were 32ft long overall and 7ft 3in wide over body, only 3in less than the then maximum permitted width for road vehicles. Looking back at that carefully planned arcade of 19 roads giving access to Sandy Row car shed, one recalls the words of a motorman: 'You couldn't get a pencil between the door pillars and the side of a "McCreary"'. The lower saloon had seats for 24 passengers: 2 and 1 transversely in four rows and a longitudinal three-seater bench in each corner. The upper saloon accommodated 28 on 2 and2 seating and a further six over each platform. Mounted on an 8ft wheelbase Maley & Taunton swing-link truck with 50hp motors, the 'McCreary' design was fully up to date with air brakes and folding entrance doors. They had all been withdrawn by the end of 1953.

Above: A 'McCreary' in its last year of service. When the Balmoral route went over to diesel buses it was thought necessary to retain trams at peak times on the Windsor Grounds short working. This soon became an all-day service! No 395, destined for Ligoniel, turns back at Windsor on 18 February 1953 as a Balmoral bus approaches.

Opposite: Drawing of a 'McCreary' car.

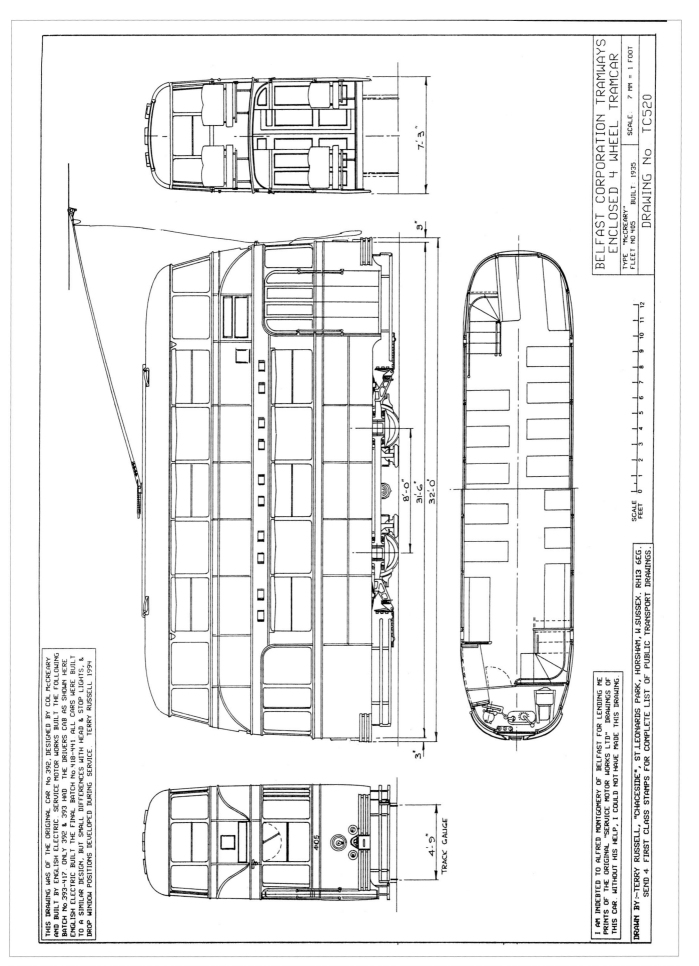

BELFAST CORPORATION TRAMWAYS
ENCLOSED 4 WHEEL TRAMCAR

TYPE "McCREARY"
FLEET No 405   BUILT 1935.   SCALE: 7 MM = 1 FOOT

DRAWING No TC520

THIS DRAWING WAS OF THE ORIGINAL CAR No 392, DESIGNED BY COL McCREARY
AND BUILT BY ENGLISH ELECTRIC. SERVICE MOTOR WORKS BUILT THE FOLLOWING
BATCH No.393-417. ONLY 392 & 393 HAD THE DRIVERS CAB AS SHOWN HERE
ENGLISH ELECTRIC BUILT THE FINAL BATCH No.418-441 ALL CARS WERE BUILT
TO A SIMILAR DESIGN, BUT SMALL DIFFERENCES WITH HEAD & STOP LIGHTS, &
DROP WINDOW POSITIONS DEVELOPED DURING SERVICE.   TERRY RUSSELL 1994

I AM INDEBTED TO ALFRED MONTGOMERY OF BELFAST FOR LENDING ME
PRINTS OF THE ORIGINAL "SERVICE MOTOR WORKS LTD" DRAWINGS OF
THIS CAR. WITHOUT HIS HELP, I COULD NOT HAVE MADE THIS DRAWING.

DRAWN BY:- TERRY RUSSELL, "CHACESIDE", ST.LEONARDS PARK, HORSHAM, W.SUSSEX. RH13 6EG.
SEND 4 FIRST CLASS STAMPS FOR COMPLETE LIST OF PUBLIC TRANSPORT DRAWINGS.

SCALE
FEET   0 1 2 3 4 5 6 7 8 9 10 11 12

7'-3"

3"

8'-0"
31'-6"
32'-0"

3"

4'-9"

TRACK GAUGE

405

Route by Route

Route numbers appear to have been allocated around 1925 and perhaps it was too late for them to be imprinted in the communal memory, for one never seems to hear somebody being advised, for instance, to 'take a number eleven to Balmoral'. It was always 'get on a Balmoral tram in front of the City Hall' etc, etc. To make matters worse, there was more than one revision of route numbers before confusion descended at the outbreak of World War 2 when trolleybus substitution was in full swing. This put an end to the general practice of through running between opposite termini, always via Castle Junction of course. To give the reader and viewer a comprehensive albeit convoluted tour of the tramway system, we shall attempt this in numerical order, using the last complete run of numbers and beginning with the city's longest route. This was covered by numbers 1 to 5.

GLENGORMLEY

Numbers 1 and 2 were given to the short workings indicated as 'Antrim Road' that turned back at Chichester Park, the old BST terminus that was end-on to the southern extremity of the Cavehill & Whitewell Tramway. In 1943 this was extended about half a mile to the crossover at Lansdowne Road. The pairing of numbers took account of alternative routes via Carlisle Circus and Duncairn Gardens respectively. The numbers 3 and 5 covered the whole distance from 'the Junction' to Glengormley, about 5 miles. In common with most other routes, Antrim Road cars were able to return without reversal, thanks to the generous provision of street-to-street connections in the city centre. The missing Route 4 was a 'short' working to Bellevue (nearly 4½ miles out and good value for the old 3d fare). Here, a 'toastrack' bus took passengers uphill to the Zoo and other family entertainments, not forgetting the Floral Hall for dancing, when late transport would be laid on. There were other Antrim Road destinations on the blinds'. 'Waterworks' was another place of resort, identified by 'ANTRIM ROAD' in small red capitals below. Further out and serviced by a crossover at Willowbank Gardens, Dunmore Park

greyhound stadium had its own place on the indicators though situated some yards down Alexandra Park Avenue, and Grays Lane crossover, 3¼ miles out, saw frequent use. The Glengormley line would have been double-track all the way to that village had it not been for the obduracy of the County Surveyor for Antrim, who refused to allow Belfast Corporation to double the Cavehill & Whitewell line beyond the city boundary. This was about a quarter-mile north of Grays Lane. The outward track obediently curved into the inward one at this point, the single track remaining off-centre of the road to Glengormley, with four passing places between the boundary and the terminal loop. The first of these was at the Bellevue entrance and 300ft short of Whitewell Road junction. The second loop was at Whitewell Post Office, the third at Elmfield House and the fourth, then in open country, some 700ft beyond that. Belfast Tramways Department had laid square setts sufficient for double track throughout, perhaps intending to obtain the necessary powers at a future date.

Below left: On 9 April 1947 No 405 is inward-bound on Route 1 at Bridge Street having negotiated the S-bend around the Belfast Bank (left background) with its blind ready-wound. The battle-scarred *Northern Whig* newspaper office behind No 405 took hard knocks in the Blitz. By then, the *Whig* was solidly Tory in outlook.

Above: Not much greenery in Duncairn Gardens on 1 November 1945 as No 342 descends towards York Street. Post-war reconstruction has still to take place after the terrible devastation this inner residential area suffered in 1941.

Left: Inward bound via Duncairn Gardens, No 386 enters York Street from Brougham Street. This was one of the junctions chosen to divert shipyard traffic from the city centre. Rush-hour cars from Queen's Road traversed a single-track curve 'wrong road' from the Whitla Street junction (out of sight on right) and regained the left-hand road on a trailing crossover. The date is 14 January 1949.

Left: Trams took their own route around Carlisle Circus to avoid Roaring Hanna's statue. Regrettably, the photographer was too concerned to catch No 373 on the Antrim Road junction and left the hell-fire preacher out of the picture, for his graven image no longer exists, a victim of the recent Troubles. It would have been nice to have him perhaps pointing a condemnatory finger at a passing 'Chamberlain'. Antrim Road with its new trolleybus overhead curves to right; there is an unfinished piece of switch-work visible. It is January 1949.

Right: This suburban shopping area on Antrim Road has grown up at the intersection of Skegoneil Avenue and Alexandra Gardens with Antrim Road. Characteristically, the shops are all single-storey and have their own lay-by. In the left background is Fortwilliam Park Presbyterian Church. On 20 January 1949 inward-bound No 434 passes the triangular trailing junctions with the branch to Salisbury Avenue tram depot.

Right: On the same day, outward-bound No 383 on Route 1 has been withdrawn from service and is entering Salisbury Avenue without reversing the trolley. One of the depot staff holds the trolley rope in case of dewirement.

Right: Salisbury Avenue depot, seen from the entrance on 20 January 1949. There were eight roads in the car shed. It can be seen that the damaged roof over roads 1-5 was replaced after the 1941 Blitz.

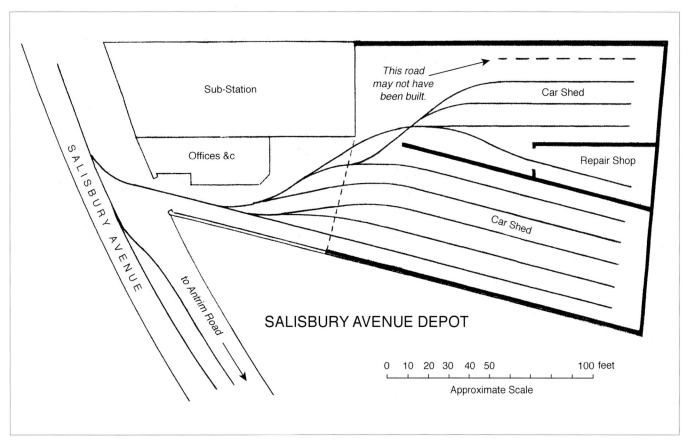

Sub-Station

Offices &c

This road may not have been built.

Car Shed

Repair Shop

Car Shed

SALISBURY AVENUE

to Antrim Road

SALISBURY AVENUE DEPOT

0 10 20 30 40 50   100 feet

Approximate Scale

Above: On the Lansdowne Road short working, No 367 is still on the outward track. The city-bound lorry has more leeway than one would think, but on this job, tram conductors need eyes in the back of their heads. 20 January 1949.

Above: Approaching Bellevue Park, the scenery on Antrim Road improves as Cave Hill encroaches on the left. The ground here is rather unstable, though tram services seem to have been unaffected. Note the extra trolleybus standards. No 371 has reversed on the Gray's Lane crossover and is returning to the city on 20 January 1949.

Above: End of track at Glengormley on 24 January 1949, the last day of Belfast's longest tram route. Rebuilt horse-tram 238 has been hired by the Belfast branch of the Irish Railway Record Society. Two notable transport enthusiasts — 'driver' Bryan Boyle and the late 'Mac' Arnold — are on the platform.

Above: Glengormley terminus, with No 354 displaying Route 3. On 12 January 1949 the village is still outside city limits and remains pleasantly 'countrified'.

Above: 'Chamberlains' Nos 354 and 365 on Glengormley terminal loop at the northernmost extremity of the Belfast tramways. Note overhead wiring leading into the new off-road trolleybus terminus. How simple it would have been to lay a terminal stub into that open space, saving on the visual mess above.

CREGAGH

By the late 1930s, Cregagh, on the south-eastern boundary of the city, was recorded as being served by Route 6 to Bellevue (Antrim Road) and Route 8 to Falls Road in west Belfast. After conversion of the latter to trolleybus operation from 28 March 1938, Route 8 was either diverted or cut back to Castle Junction. In the previous 18 months the first tramway closure since Ormeau Avenue (1913) had occurred. It involved abandonment of the last half-mile or so of the tramway on Cregagh Road, from Bell's Bridge, on 1 October 1936. And the new streamlined trams were still being delivered! It is hard to understand so much untidy thinking. A duplicate omnibus service, at a higher fare, ran to the old tram terminus. Worn-out trackwork was blamed. Was this a legacy of Chamberlain's regime? He was not a bigoted tram enthusiast, even though a class of 50 trams was named after him. His relations with the Transport Committee had not been good — he sued one member for libel — but it looks as if he wanted to make economies. Chamberlain was also accused of neglecting the Corporation omnibuses.

GREENCASTLE–BALMORAL

Routes 9 and 10 terminated at the city boundary on Shore Road; 9 had come from Falls Road and 10 from Balmoral. By World War 2 the Greencastle service commenced from the city centre and had a short working labelled 'Fortwilliam Shore Road' a destination also carried by cars returning to Shore Road depot.

Left: This is Bell's Bridge, formerly a short working on Route 8 but now the Cregagh terminus. The parapet of Bell's Bridge is immediately on the right of the car, No 403. Rails and overhead continue towards the Cregagh Hills in the background. Both crew members watch the photographer from the rear platform before the trolley is turned. Note the 'message boy', as they were called here, propelling his delivery bike. His necktie and neat haircut are seldom found on any young person today, irrespective of class. Trolleybuses reached Cregagh on 13 February 1941. *John Kennedy collection*

Right: This is Castle Junction on 29 September 1950. The eastern fork of the junction is visible behind No 407, which is on the Fortwilliam working. Geographically, we are in Castle Place, with High Street curving away in the background. The trolleybus is outside Robb's department store, with the massive Burton/Woolworth building opposite. Every emporium in sight has since been rebuilt, changed hands, or both. Note the spring-operated crossover points for quick reversal when needed.

Left: Inward-bound No 322 enters High Street from Bridge Street on 28 September 1950. The blitzed site of Arnott's store on the right has become a temporary car park but the store will be rebuilt in the next couple of years.

Above: A scene in York Street on 14 January 1949. Inward bound from Antrim Road via Duncairn Gardens, No 434 has emerged from Brougham Street while its sister from Greencastle comes up in the rear. The leading car must have had precedence; trams ran to a much tighter timetable than we thought, and the drivers of vehicles running 'in predestinate grooves' had a very good knowledge of clearances. The Shore Road line is still waiting for its trolleybus wiring.

Right: No 287 on the Fortwilliam Park short working on 7 November 1949 is returning to the city but the 'Donegall Pass' indicator tells us that its ultimate destination is Sandy Row depot.

Left: Newly erected trolleybus overhead is visible as No 429 passes Shore Road depot on an inward run to an illegible destination. The 'prefabs' in the rear are the asbestos-cement variety that lasted many years longer than expected. It is 7 November 1949.

Right: A late 1930s view of No 365 (displaying Route 10 for Balmoral) at Greencastle shows that the terminal stub turned inwards to disembark passengers at the kerbside. At some time in the 1940s this was removed and a crossover installed on the double track a few yards short of the original terminus. Mount Street joined the Shore Road behind the car. *John Kennedy collection*

Right: Pioneer 'rebuild' No 164 is at Fortwilliam, which is still a tram terminus on the converted Greencastle route. Note the tram overhead merging with the positive trolleybus wire beyond No 164. The date is 25 May 1952.

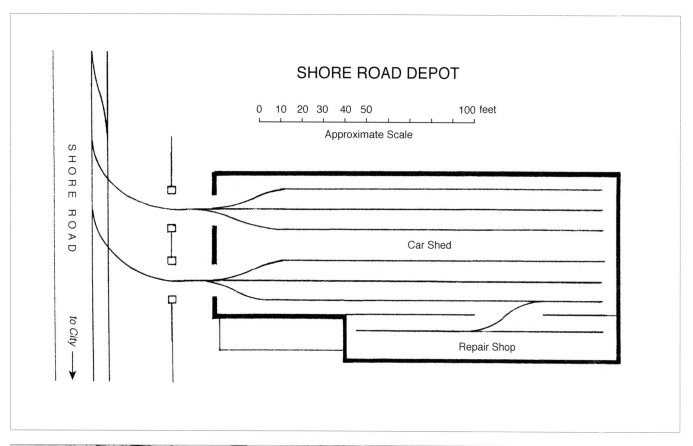

SHORE ROAD DEPOT

0 10 20 30 40 50   100 feet

Approximate Scale

SHORE ROAD

to City ⟶

Car Shed

Repair Shop

Above: Coming out of Bedford Street at the Ormeau Avenue end, No 394 takes the curve into Dublin Road bearing what seems to be the destination 'Marlb(orough) Park'. Random patterns of iron-hard square setts decorate the foreground. Rather before our time, the abandoned Ormeau Avenue tracks had branched to the right. The date is 9 October 1952.

Left: The tramlines didn't penetrate very far into Sandy Row. They are seen turning left down Gaffikin Street to the 19-road car shed; Napier Street and its tram workshops run alongside but behind the camera. All this was accessed by a double-track Y-junction from Lisburn Road. This was the day of a tram tour around Belfast, hence the presence of pioneer 'rebuild' No 164 on 25 May 1952.

Above: Looking city-wards on Lisburn Road, No 395 has reversed on 'Windsor Grounds' crossover. The remainder of Lisburn Road is now tramless, but to ease the pain perhaps, the Department continues to operate a short working to Windsor Park, the residential road seen on the right. The indicator destination was something of a misnomer, the 'Blues' ground (Linfield) being on the far side of the railway, a longish walk over Tate's Avenue bridge and to confuse matters was also called Windsor Park. The date is 18 February 1953.

Left: Marlborough Park was the original short working for both Lisburn and Malone Roads. Older indicator blinds had one road name in red and the other in green, but I cannot recall which was which! Here is No 22, one of the few rebuilds given level upper-deck window sills all round, reversing at the Lisburn Road crossover on a sunny July day in 1947.

Left: On an almost empty Lisburn Road on 25 May 1952, No 164 prepares to return city-wards at the King's Hall crossover just beyond the Stockman's Lane-Balmoral Avenue crossroads in rear of the car. With everything from agricultural shows to ice-skating, Ideal Homes exhibitions and mass entertainment, the Hall, owned by the Royal Ulster Agricultural Society, gave the Balmoral route good business through the year.

Right: The 1930s-style of King's Hall façade is visible in this view of Balmoral terminus. By now (24 October 1952) trams like No 384 are showing their age. However, unlike other undertakings hell-bent on abandonment, an element of civic pride had Belfast Transport Department repaint a number of 'Chamberlains' around this time.

Left: Another aspect of Balmoral terminus, with Nos 386 and 329 and an inspector giving orders, or laying down the law? The date is 1 November 1952. End of track was right on the city boundary.

FALLS DEPOT

Below: Having visited Cregagh and Greencastle, the opposite termini of which were both at Falls Road, the unfortunate fact is our complete lack of photographs showing tramcar activity on any part of the Falls Road route. Tracks ended at Fruithill Park, outside the city boundary and half a mile beyond the Falls depot at Andersonstown. Just short of the fork where Glen Road meets Falls Road, this car shed was the most noticeable on the Belfast system. On the 1932 Ordnance Survey map, the building scales 500ft long and 125ft wide. About 370ft of this length was accounted for by the fitting-out shed for the 170 new tramcars coming from the Brush Co. Its later use is unknown until c1926 when it became the Department's motor-omnibus depot and workshop, for which there was an entrance in Divis Drive. It has since been altered following two fires. The rebuilding uncovered some interesting archaeology: the lightweight rails on which the1905 electric cars were assembled had been concreted over when the buses came. The track fan in front of Falls depot remained in situ for many years, revealing some anomalies that are indicated on the plan (right). *John Kennedy collection*

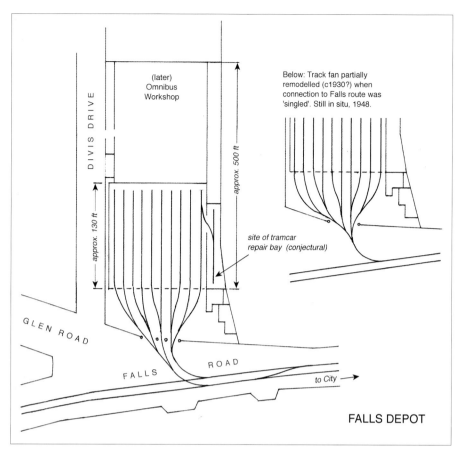

Below: Track fan partially remodelled (c1930?) when connection to Falls route was 'singled'. Still in situ, 1948.

site of tramcar repair bay (conjectural)

FALLS DEPOT

DUNDONALD

Another lengthy route shared numbers 11 and 12 with the Lisburn Road line to Balmoral, giving a through route from east to south-west. In this case Balmoral-Dundonald was Route 11 via Bedford Street and Queen's Bridge, while in the reverse direction Route 12 went by Queen's Bridge and Great Victoria Street. Dundonald via Albert Bridge was Route 13 but memories are uncertain as to its westernmost destination. Trolleybuses were introduced on the Dundonald leg as from 16 November 1942 (via Queen's Bridge) and 8 March 1943 (via Albert Bridge). Personal recollections of the Queen's Bridge route were that trolleybus frequencies were augmented by a tram service, usually the old red cars, from the city to Ballyhackamore on Upper Newtownards Road, but both tram routes remained intact as far as Knock Road to the late 1940s. It was necessary to retain Knock depot to house trams still required for the enormous peak-hour traffic. There was one important crossover on Lower Newtownards Road at Gawn Street, which came to life in the football season. The destination blinds said 'Oval Gds'. The Oval was home ground to Glentoran FC, deadly rivals to Linfield at Windsor Park and close to the BCDR Bangor line. It entailed something of a walk from the Newtownards Road tram stop. 'Connswater' was another east Belfast short working. Until closure of the Stormont tramway it had used a crossover on the Holywood Road line close to the 'Holywood Arches' where the BCDR main line crossed the former road and the Upper Newtownards Road on a pair of girder bridges (there were never any arches!). Connswater cars then reversed at the equivalent crossover on the Knock line. They were eventually displaced when a turning loop for trolleybuses was made in Grampian Avenue, between the two main roads. The Ballyhackamore crossover at Earlswood Road featured in a court case c1946 involving a tramcar. The Resident Magistrate was understandably baffled when he was told that the tram was being shunted from one side to the other at Knock depot. The Knock crossover was unserviceable and the 'shunt' involved a trip of about half a mile.

The other leg of the Dundonald route, via Albertbridge Road became the only means of access to Mountpottinger depot when the Castlereagh service was diverted on abandonment of the Mountpottinger Road tracks in 1937. Most of the elaborate scissors junction at the Mount remained in use to retain depot access. Pointwork here had grooved movable tongues, not seen elsewhere in Belfast though widely used in Dublin. The isolation of Mountpottinger depot from Queen's Road led to construction circa 1942 of a 'hairpin' single-track spur at the 'Ropeworks Corner' where the Albertbridge Road joins the Newtownards Road.

Above: A masterpiece of planning on a restricted site? There were 17 parallel roads under cover in Mountpottinger depot as well as a repair shop accessible from the last road on the right. All of this, with a very short forecourt to accommodate the 'depot fan' seen in the foreground. The tangled mass of manganese steel was no doubt the work of one of the Sheffield giants, Edgar Allen, Hadfields or Osborne's Titan Trackwork. The date is 6 June 1953.

Above: When Mountpottinger depot was visited in June 1953, this 'McCreary' and the trio of 'Rebuilds' were all examples of fast-disappearing classes and mainly used for shipyard traffic at rush hours.

Left: The 'Ropeworks Corner' was where the two routes to Dundonald via Newtownards Road and Albertbridge Road joined at an acute angle. On the hairpin bend between the two roads there was just enough radius to put in the curve upon which No 164 is standing on 25 May 1952. As explained earlier, this restored the through running from Mountpottinger depot to Queen's Road that had been lost when the tracks on Mountpottinger Road had been lifted in 1937.

Above: The entrance to Knock depot is seen from the Newtownards Road on 9 May 1947. The depot foreman at this time was a Mr Forbes. His staff willingly fetched cars from the shed for photography without complaint. As a result, the forecourt might look quite untidy at times! There had been 17 roads in the car shed but that on the extreme left had been disconnected, one of seven that were shorter than the others as a large workshop lay behind them. The six centre roads were the longest, whilst three of the four remaining tracks extended into another repair shop at the rear. This facility was bigger that than at Mountpottinger and may have helped to prolong the life of Knock depot.

Above: Several of the converted horse-cars were shedded at Knock. Being used only at peak times, they kept their looks better than the usually battered 'standard reds'. Here is No 227, 9 May 1947, showing the characteristic rocker panels that identified these cars.

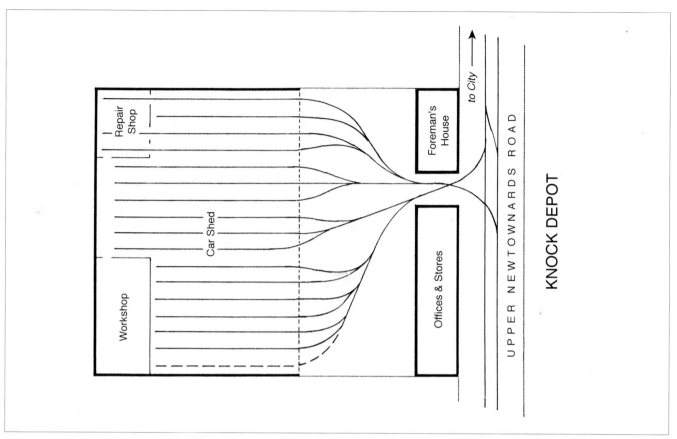

KNOCK DEPOT

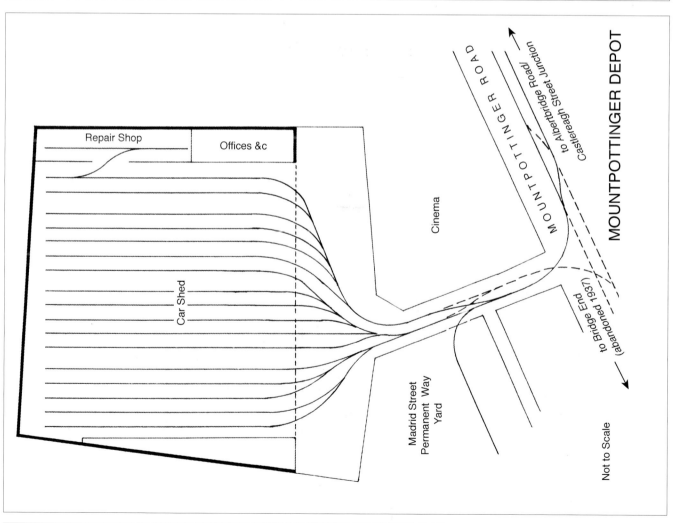

MOUNTPOTTINGER DEPOT

Above: Another 'Conversion' is captured at Knock on 6 May 1946: No 223 is still carrying the ornamental wrought-ironwork applied to the platforms when they first appeared as uncanopied electric open-toppers in 1905.

Above: Blame wartime censorship for having nothing later than this 1930s view of Dundonald tram terminus, but its surroundings remained unchanged when the trolleybuses came. Their turning place was the Elk Inn, a matter of yards (or metres if you wish) beyond the tramlines, where the Newtownards and Comber roads bifurcated. No 369 is bound for Balmoral via Queen's Bridge. *John Kennedy collection*

CLIFTONVILLE

The area of north-west Belfast was a late-19th century development said to be modelled on the upper-crust suburb of Bristol called Clifton. The Cliftonville Road tramway branched off the Antrim Road line a short distance south of Duncairn Gardens, climbing a fairly steep gradient to join the Oldpark route at the latter's terminus. The route number 14 had been used by an Ormeau Road-Cliftonville service later cut back to Castle Junction. The Oldpark and Cliftonville routes met by means of a double junction which was simplified to a single-track connection on the outward lines. Cliftonville cars reversed short of this junction, on their own crossover. Oldpark Road beckoned invitingly, empty of rails, beyond here but it was trolleybus overhead that was to cater for post-war development of the Carr's Glen district on the slopes of Cave Hill. This 'combined' terminus was useful one rush-hour when a serious blockage of Antrim Road diverted Glengormley cars on the Carlisle Circus route, with two reversals, of course. Some Glengormley folk got good value for their 3d that evening. Cliftonville trams were replaced by motor-buses with effect from 1 September 1947. The Carr's Glen trolleybuses did not materialise until 1951.

ORMEAU ROAD AND RAVENHILL

There were three different routes to the Ormeau Road terminus at Galwally Park until 1940 and the numbers 15-19 and 21 had all been allocated to their permutations. At one time a cross-town service from Cliftonville using 1 and 16 ran via Botanic Avenue and Cromac Street respectively. By World War 2 Routes 15 and 16 were running from Castle Junction, but the quiet 15, traversing decent inner suburbia in the University and Assembly's College area, was a wartime victim of essential sewerage works that severed the tracks permanently after motor-bus substitution in 1944. The remaining Cromac Street line had Belfast gasworks (famous for its profitable by-products) along one side almost to the Ormeau Bridge that was Belfast's third road crossing over the Lagan. Once over the bridge, there was the Ormeau Park, gift of the Marquess of Donegall to the City, on the east side and later suburbia around Ballynafeigh. Passing Rosetta, where the Ravenhill line joined, the Ormeau Road terminus was at Galwally Park. It had been cut back a few yards from the junction of Newtownbreda Road and Church Road.

The 'UC Grounds' short working form Castle Junction was numbered 17 (via Cromac Street) and 18 (Botanic Avenue) and turned trolleys at the Agincourt Avenue crossover on Ormeau Road, not far beyond University Avenue where the Botanic route joined. Incidentally, the initials stood for Ulster Cricket Grounds, a sports area at the riverside about half-way between the Central Railway bridge and Ormeau Bridge.

Ravenhill Road diverged south from Albertbridge Road immediately beyond the Albert Bridge and for most of its course ran in a straight line to its junction with Ormeau Road at Rosetta. In consequence, it did not tap a large residential area, but the liberal tramways management had in the 1930s assigned route number 18 to Donegall Road-Ravenhill Road working, while 19 and 21 covered Springfield-Ravenhill Park, the latter point being half a mile short of the Rosetta crossover. When Ravenhill went over to motor buses in 1940 UC Grounds was awarded numbers 17 and 18. Before abandonment, every alternate Ravenhill tram was running to the Ormeau Road terminus. How this was indicated on the cars is unknown to us.

Above: Cliftonville terminus in July 1946, with No 89 (the Hen-House) being turned. Tracks on the left led to Oldpark terminus. The area was know locally as Cliftonville Circus though at that time the name does not seem to have been used officially. Reverting to No 89, Mike Maybin, chronicler of Belfast's transport, has determined that the design and enclosure of what had been a 'Standard' car was carried out in 1923 under Mr Vernon, rolling stock engineer, during the interregnum following Mr Moffett's resignation.

Right: Here is No 123 on a UC Grounds short working, 14 April 1948. The two rebuilds are doing a sort of symmetrical ballet manoeuvre, one entering and one leaving Donegall Place on the Donegall Square North curves.

Left: The Chichester Street-Victoria Street triangular junction is seen on 9 April 1948, with No 296 about to turn right into Victoria Street for Ormeau via Cromac Street. The cityscape behind the 'Moffett' is now unrecognisable. The buildings you see were replaced in the 1950s and 1960s — now the latter have been demolished prior to vast redevelopment.

Right: The 'Moffetts' seem to have had a near monopoly on the No 16 service in the weeks before trolleybus take-over. In this Cromac Square view of 9 April 1948, No 315 has negotiated the East Bridge Street junction. Much has changed here. Even Telephone House in the left background, a building still new in 1939, has since had a substantial enlargement.

Left: At the UC Grounds crossover on 3 October 1946, the conductor of No 153 swings the trolley around while a blurred Bedford OWB utility single-decker scuttles past. Belfast Corporation had a generous allocation of these buses.

Right: Passengers dismount from No 300 at Ormeau Road terminus on 6 April 1948. Surprisingly, the indicator blind has been wound to 'Antrim Road'. In the distance, at Rosetta, Ormeau Road inclines left, with the former Ravenhill tram route going straight ahead.

Left: The 'McCreary' (No 411) at Ormeau terminus is on Route 15 via Bedford Street. This 1930s scene gives us our only glimpse of a Ravenhill car, No 267. Why both cars have their trolleys on the 'inward' wire yet are on the city-wards side of the reversing crossover, is a minor mystery. Likewise, the '20' on 267 seems to be an error. *John Kennedy collection*

Right: The Albert Clock says twenty to two on 9 April 1948 as No 279 returns to Queen's Road on the lunchtime workings from UC Grounds. It is on the facing crossover in Victoria Street and is about to negotiate the single-track curve into Ann Street, no doubt to the dismay of any motorist not au fait with this occurrence.

Above: Five days later, one of the dwindling band of red cars, No 61, performs the same operation and is about to resume left-hand running as it reaches the Ann Street trailing crossover. This was the last example of several such curves introduced by J. S. D. Moffett in his short stay as General Manager, to reduce congestion at 'the Junction'. This part of Victoria Street behind 61 is almost devoid of buildings since the 1941 Blitz. The 'east' end of St George's Church on High Street can be seen as a result. Its orientation is north-south.

Above: Putting the finishing touches to trolleybus overhead on the Knockbreda extension in April 1948. Such extensions were very often operational necessities in order to find turning places for trackless vehicles. And they talk about the inflexibility of trams . . . however we include this view for the sake of the veteran AZ 140, superannuated to tower wagon and essential back-up for both trams and trolleybuses.

Below: On the last day of the Bloomfield tram route, No 178 is using the Cregagh trolleybus wire in Woodstock Street as it prepares to join Albertbridge Road on its way to the Junction. It is 5 May 1946.

BLOOMFIELD

A service between Bloomfield in East Belfast and Donegall Road, numbered 20, had been recorded as long ago as 1930. The western terminus later shifted to Springfield, but cross-city running ended when it was decided to convert all east Belfast tram routes as a preliminary to complete substitution by trolleybuses. To a stranger in Belfast it was a fascinating quest to ascertain what tram routes still remained east of the Lagan. In 1942 the Bloomfield tram was found to negotiate the Mountpottinger junctions and run by Castlereagh Street, where there had been another of those scissor arrangements at the divergence of Beersbridge Road and Castlereagh Road. With the coming of trolleybuses to Castlereagh this was simplified to one double junction. This diversion was only a temporary measure while the lower end of Beersbridge Road was being rewired; normal route for Bloomfield trams and trolleybuses was via Woodstock Street, thence turning left from the Cregagh route. The Castlereagh Street complex was reduced to a single-line connection facing for incoming cars that allowed access to Mountpottinger depot in the final years of the Bloomfield trams.

Above: The view of Bloomfield terminus as seen from North Road on 27 March 1946. The trolleybus turning circle is in position. From here and to the right, trolleybus standards were erected along North Road to where it met Newtownards Road but were never used.

Right: On the outward track at Bloomfield, No 294 awaits its turn to draw ahead to the reversal point. The date is 27 March 1946.

Above: Goodbye to the North Road tram: another angle on Bloomfield terminal stub on the last day, this time facing towards North Road. Street furniture includes the tramwaymen's urinal on the traffic island, and a communal air-raid shelter on right. The latter seemed to take an age to demolish.

Left: Red car No 43 and a 'Moffett' at Springfield terminus in July 1946. The driver of No 43 claimed her to be Belfast's first top-covered car and folk memory should not always be discounted. A picture-postcard exists with just such a title; the broadside view (no visible number) shows an overall roof supported on iron pillars, and a complete lack of glazing on the upper deck. Conventional top covering in Belfast began in 1907 when the uncommon 'short-top saloon' balcony car was introduced but No 43 is one of a random handful having three full-length windows. Note also the horizontal panelling below the upper window sills meaning less depth of glass. This unique feature was also pointed out by our informant.

SPRINGFIELD

One of the most important tram routes in Belfast, judging by the service offered and the fact that it lasted until November 1952, Route 21 from Springfield in west Belfast extended to several different termini as traffic patterns shifted in the long drawn out abandonment programme. Springfield Road had both mass housing and heavy industry on its doorstep, as it were, as well as the inevitable shipyard traffic to and from Queen's Road. Cross-town destinations had included the latter on an all-day basis and also Oldpark and Ravenhill, some of course involving other route numbers. The illustrations in this section include trams carrying post-war numbers which the reader is requested to ignore! Not quite half-way along Grosvenor Road, the Distillery Street crossover provided a reversing point for football specials. The distillery was Dunville's, the soccer club 'Distillery' and indicator blinds said 'Distillery Grounds'.

Top: 'Rebuild' No 287 reversing on the Springfield terminal stub. It is 15 October 1952 and the destination 'Ballygomartin' will be noticed. Two 'Chamberlains' and a 'Moffett' have clustered beyond the 'inward' boarding point, two of them probably preparing for a shift-change at Mackie's engineering works.

Above: No 260 awaits departure from Springfield on 15 October 1952. This fine autumn day was an incentive to photography in an otherwise dreary part of the city.

Left: No 336 and another 'Moffett', No 330, have reached the top of Grosvenor Road on their way to Springfield. Dunville Park is on the left and the famous Royal Victoria Hospital out of sight on right. Here the Springfield cars cross the Falls trolleybus route.

Left: Policemen on 'point duty' still controlled traffic on busy intersections outside the city centre. On 15 October 1952, city-bound Springfield car, its ultimate destination Crumlin Road, crosses Falls Road. Prior to 1938 there were two double-track curves (half a 'Grand Union') connecting these two tram routes.

Left: The Ritz Cinema with John Wayne's enigmatic portrait creates this period piece. A pristine No 356 causes a fine clatter on the crossing at it leaves Howard Street and heads for 'the Grosvenor' to commence a steady climb to Springfield on 11 September 1952. Incidentally, the rival Hippodrome's awning is just glimpsed on the opposite corner. We are in Belfast's entertainment centre.

Opposite above: **From the opposite corner to the last view, we are looking up Howard Street to the City Hall. On the left is seen Church House, headquarters of the Presbyterian Church in Ireland. No 407 makes a fine sight as she sails across the 'half Grand Union' here.**

Opposite below: **Sir Alfred Brumwell Thomas's City Hall, completed a year after the electrification on Belfast's tramways, seldom figures in photographs of the latter, for the simple reason that the trams themselves passed by the north and west of Donegall Square, from where one would be 'looking into the sun' most of the time. Smog permitting of course. The west flank of that edifice is behind No 371 as she turns into Howard Street. The Bedford Street tracks go straight ahead.**

Above left: **One of the most familiar views in central Belfast, Donegall Square North on 16 October 1952. No 378 on the Springfield run is turning into Donegall Square West. We could have done with more of those traffic islands that allowed tram passengers to board and alight safely. The time on Robinson & Cleaver's clock reminds the photographer as to how he spent his lunch hour on 16 October 1952.**

Left: **Surprisingly, this view of Donegall Place from another of those islands finds traffic levels moderate; trams have almost a monopoly of public transport but the street is dotted with jay-walking pedestrians as far as you can see. No 407 heads for Springfield on 16 October 1952.**

Left: **On the last day of May 1950, route number 21 is still in use on Springfield cars. No 341 is on the reversing crossover at Crumlin Road, Ardoyne. The double-line branch from Ardoyne depot comes in on the right of the tram. We are looking south-east towards Holy Cross RC Church.**

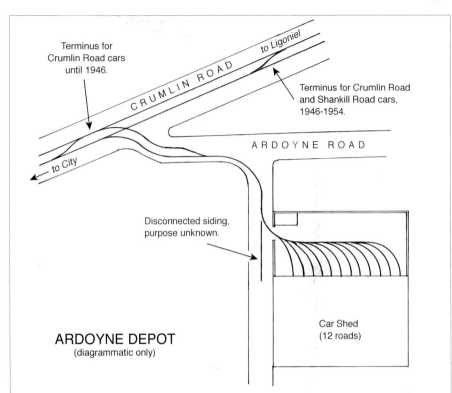

Terminus for
Crumlin Road cars
until 1946.

CRUMLIN ROAD

to Ligoniel

Terminus for Crumlin Road
and Shankill Road cars,
1946-1954.

to City

ARDOYNE ROAD

Disconnected siding,
purpose unknown.

Car Shed
(12 roads)

ARDOYNE DEPOT
(diagrammatic only)

CASTLEREAGH-OLDPARK

Another cross-city route that was severed by trolleybus substitution previously made use of numbers 22 and 24. Castlereagh, in east Belfast, was accessible by both Queen's and Albert Bridges, the former route branching from the Newtownards Road line at Bridge End to go by Mountpottinger Road and the scissors junctions already mentioned. It was at the first of these that the two routes converged. The sudden abandonment of worn-out track on Mountpottinger Road in 1937 left Albert Bridge as the only means of access to Castlereagh, but when conversion came on 5 June 1941 only the Queen's Bridge was used by Castlereagh trolleybuses. Oldpark continued to be served by trams until 30 April 1951, being linked to Springfield by the city centre. The outer termini were both in west Belfast.

Above: The Castlereagh terminus was at Houston Park, hidden by No 330 in this pre-World War 2 view. Displaying route 24 on a card at the entrance as well as the indicator, 330 carries her fully lined livery. The side-board reads 'via Castlereagh St, Albert Bridge & Clifton Street'. Trolleybuses would have a turning place at Houston Park but the terminus was extended to the Knock Road crossroads, otherwise the 'Hill Foot Road'. *John Kennedy collection*

Above: **This is where Oldpark Road meets Crumlin Road (on left). The crossover for 'Agnes Street Crumlin Road' short working is out of sight a few yards to right. On 25 April 1951 No 422 is city-bound from Oldpark.**

Left: **Without No 438, this view could have been in the West Riding of Yorkshire: bare moorland rising to the Pennines and a mill chimney for good measure. It is, of course, Oldpark Road in the last days of its tram service.**

Above: When trolleybuses invaded Cliftonville Road and extended the service to Carr's Glen a turning circle was provided at the 'Circus' and the Oldpark trams were pushed back to a new crossover on Oldpark Road. Here, No 318 has her trolley on the inward wire and will be going to Springfield via the Junction. It is 25 April 1951.

Above: A group of cars, Nos 438, 401 and what must be 318 behind, gather at Oldpark terminus on the same day as the previous photograph.

QUEEN'S ROAD

The all-day service from City Hall to Queen's Island had been allocated number 23. It also passed Queen's Quay terminus of the Belfast & Co Down Railway, with its own under-cover siding and regular workings to and from the Northern Counties station at York Road. Cars worked to the railway timetables and had their own printed tables at each terminus. It was a pity that the same facility was never provided at Great Victoria Street station, but it would not be a surprise to find that tram crews on that route were aware of train times. The writer recalls being anxious about getting the last Bangor train one night, but the conductor of the Queen's Road car he had boarded was quite reassuring; he was well aware of its departure time.

Above right: On 13 May 1950 rebuilt 256 has just crossed Queen's Bridge and passes under a tangle of feeder cables serving both trams and trolleybuses. The conductor dutifully signals its intention to make a left turn into Station Street. The short length of tramway in the latter thoroughfare was originally the property of the Belfast & Co Down Railway, but worked exclusively by Belfast Street Tramways Co and its municipal successor. *H. C. Casserley*

Right: Having mentioned City Hall as a starting point for the 'Island', we are contradicted by the late view of No 290 on the north side of Castle Junction (21 October 1952). There is no driver in sight. The Inspectors' Office is the modest kiosk half-eclipsed by the 'keep left except trams' sign on the left. The Bank Buildings in the background have changed hands more than once since.

Left: The photograph from the opposite side of Scrabo Street taken on 14 May 1950 gives a good view of the 'tram bay' in the concourse of Queen's Quay station (Belfast & Co Down Railway). A 'Chamberlain' has just arrived.
H. C. Casserley

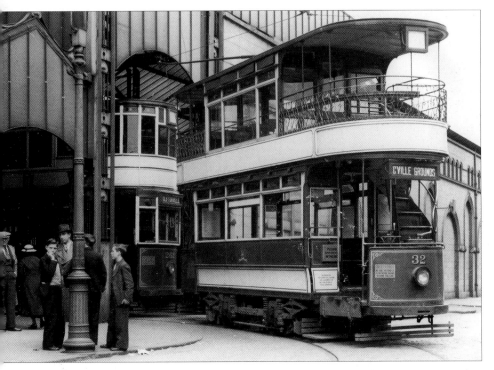

Above: A fascinating picture of 1930s Belfast. It must be Saturday: both cars visible on the Queen's Quay station siding carry Cliftonville destinations, and Cliftonville, the only amateur side in the Irish League, are at home to Bangor. Probably not Ards, for with a shorter journey the NIRTB buses are siphoning off the BCDR passenger traffic. The rebuilt station is hardly more than 25 years old and the patent glazing still looks in very good condition. *John Kennedy collection*

Above: On 6 May 1953 an inward-bound 'Chamberlain' on Queen's Road will soon be stamping over the triple railway crossing in the foreground. Rail-borne coal from the Abercorn Basin (left) passed this way.

Above: The view over the coal quays is from Scrabo Street and car No 111 is clear of the Queen's Road line waiting for a space on the station siding. This is one of the red cars given a long-wheelbase truck with half-elliptical springs. The date is 18 July 1947.

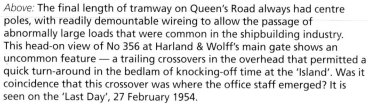

Above: The final length of tramway on Queen's Road always had centre poles, with readily demountable wireing to allow the passage of abnormally large loads that were common in the shipbuilding industry. This head-on view of No 356 at Harland & Wolff's main gate shows an uncommon feature — a trailing crossovers in the overhead that permitted a quick turn-around in the bedlam of knocking-off time at the 'Island'. Was it coincidence that this crossover was where the office staff emerged? It is seen on the 'Last Day', 27 February 1954.

Left and above right : Two aspects of No 164, the pioneer 'rebuild' at the end of the track on Queen's Road. A 5ft 3in gauge railway ran parallel to the tramway. A siding from the shipyard cuts across the tramlines at this point. The giant floating crane in the distance was 'reparations' following World War 1. The date is 25 May 1952.

STORMONT

One of the original electric routes had been that from the Holywood Arches (Upper Newtownards Road) going by Holywood Road, Belmont Road and Ballymiscaw Road to a junction with the Old Holywood Road; the latter took a hillside course, no doubt laid out at a time when the shore of Belfast Lough was impassable. The destination 'Belmont' was carried on the trams. When the Stormont Estate had been chosen as the site for Northern Ireland's Parliament Building (the latter would also house a large proportion of the NI Civil Service), the Corporation realised that further peak-hour traffic would be generated, though less boisterous than that seen on Queen's Road. The Belmont tram route was extended along Massey Avenue to Stormont Gates, half a mile away, came into use in September 1923 and had a life of less than 20 years. The replacement trolleybuses outshone the poor old trams by going through Stormont Gates to Carson's statue from where they circumnavigated Parliament Buildings. The author dreams of bogie trams humming through the greensward to a discreet terminus at the back of Stormont, leaving Carson in peace.

NORTHERN COUNTIES STATION–STRANMILLIS VIA CORPORATION STREET

This was Route 27 and the indicators said 'LMS RLY NCC'. These cars turned in Whitla Street and had no connection with the tram siding into the station, though the double track formerly curved to a junction with the York Road-Greencastle line. From Whitla Street the 27 turned south into Garmoyle Street and Corporation Street, largely given over to dockside commerce and builders' suppliers. We shall follow its course from where it turns at the Albert Clock into High Street and through Castle Junction, southward to its Laganside terminus. Motor-buses took over the northern half on 21 August 1950 and the remainder almost a year later.

Below: The tram terminus at Stormont Gates, Massey Avenue, Route 25 displayed by No 372 went across the Lagan to Stranmillis. The return working was Route 26! Note that the Belmont destination is partly visible on the blind. We are advised that there had also been a Strandtown short working and that the number 28 was used by an Oldpark-Stormont service. Behind the camera, there still exists a bank specially built to permit civil servants to cash pay-cheques without spending the entire lunch-hour going further afield. Not every 'man (or woman) from the Ministry' preferred the isolation of Stormont. *John Kennedy collection*

Right above: A prospect of Whitla Street: two tram termini in the one picture. In this 1930s view we are looking from York Road with the NCC station on the left. Belfast's second electric tramcar rests under cover in its siding. The 'Chamberlain', believed to be No 369, will turn at the adjacent crossover and proceed to the quietude of Stranmillis. The elaborate frontage of York Road station was begun by Sir Charles Lanyon and completed by the BNCR/NCC engineer Berkeley Wise, who added the Midland Hotel and tram bay. It suffered terrible destruction in 1941. If this had happened on the Continent it would have been restored in its entirety. *John Kennedy collection*

Right below: This scene, where Corporation Street bends right to become Victoria Street, shows No 238 about to reverse its trolley before taking its party on a farewell trip to Glengormley on 24 January 1949. Corporation Street was a good place to park a tram on a quiet Sunday.

Right: **Shaftesbury Square** was arguably the second most important tramway junction in Belfast. Out of sight on the left of this northward view was the junction with Donegall Road, at the corner of Bradbury Place. On a November day of fitful sunshine in 1945, No 295, having just negotiated the Botanic Avenue crossing, heads for Dublin Road en route for York Road station. The junction, complete with overhead, is still intact following the previous year's closure. Suspension of the wiring over such a large area, in all directions, is a credit to the linesmen concerned. Note the tram stop in the very middle of all this. Without the discipline of trams, Shaftesbury Square became a chaotic nightmare to which several solutions were applied.

Right: **Gradients on Stranmillis Road** are variable! No 313 climbs past what is now the Ulster Museum on 16 July 1951. The 'Moffett' had passed Queen's University and turned aside from Malone Road. Summit of the ascent would be in the vicinity of St Bartholomew's Church, followed by a sinuous descent to the Laganside. The spire on the left of our picture looks like being a formidable defence against paratroopers. It belonged to Elmwood Presbyterian Church (and is now part of the University campus).

Right: In leafy suburbia, No 360 is seen on the S-bends of Stranmillis Road. Wooded greenery to left occupies the grounds of both Stranmillis College and Riddell Hall. Belfast red brick colours the right background and those nasty but useful asbestos-cement prefabs have been built on spare ground near the river.

Above: On the same day as the previous picture, No 379 (chased by a 'McCreary') is leaving Stranmillis Road to enter Lockview Road, a convenient cul-de-sac for a tram terminus and one that cannot hinder traffic on a main road. Stranmillis Embankment comes in on the right, having followed the river from Ormeau Bridge.

Left: End of the track for No 434 in Lockview Road. The double track had continued for a further 86yd but was pruned back at an unknown date. In a seemingly petty economy, the overhead was carried on to a feeder pillar at the old terminus. Note the variety of route numbers in these Stranmillis photographs, reorganised in February 1951 to separate trolleybuses, trams and motor-buses, and promptly forgotten by the public. Queen's Road was one of the alternative termini chosen when Corporation Street was abandoned.

BALLYGOMARTIN–MALONE ROAD

With the Ballygomartin extension of 23 July 1925 the Belfast tramways reached their maximum mileage. The new line branched from the Shankill Road at Woodvale Park and was a mere 700yd long. While it was useful in serving post-war housing, the district continued to expand. It would not have been over-adventurous to extend a further mile or so. However, sectarian divisions may well have been foreseen even then. Note the curious fact that the chosen destination of Ballygomartin trams was that upper-class bastion of respectability, the Malone Road, and this continued until replacement of Malone Road trams by motor buses on 5 November 1951. Springfield became a useful alternative destination for Ballygomartin cars. The two termini were half a mile apart and there might once have been a west Belfast circular route if demography had been different. The new arrangement lasted only a year before both were replaced by motor buses. Trolleybuses by now were well and truly off the Corporation's agenda. Route numbers on this cross-town service had been 30 and 31, to Malone via Bedford Street and Great Victoria Street respectively, while that recurring annoyance of a different number for the opposite direction saw 33 being used by cars on both alternative routes to Ballygomartin.

Top: Ballygomartin terminus on Sunday 25 May 1952. The conductor of No 389 swings the trolley while No 164 on its tour of remaining tram routes waits in the background.

Above: From a different angle, No 324 comes to a halt while a 'McCreary' heads for Woodvale and the Shankill on 24 October 1952.

Left: Leaving Ballygomartin Road, No 362 slows for the junction with Woodvale Road, 24 October 1952. The gothic edifice is Woodvale Presbyterian Church.

Left: In the outward direction, No 438 eases around the corner into Ballygomartin Road. West Belfast has its fair share of hills and Enfield Street behind the car would do credit to a mining town in South Wales. The date is 24 October 1952.

Left: Looking up Woodvale Road towards Ardoyne, with No 422 on the junction. Passengers step boldly on to the roadway as the 'McCreary' approaches their stop. 24 October 1952.

Left: Our last view of a Ballygomartin tram shows No 31, rather work-worn, crossing into Howard Street from Grosvenor Road on 21 October 1952.

Right: Outward-bound for Malone Road, No 297 clears the junction with the Balmoral route in Bradbury Place on 3 November 1951.

Left: No 330 about to rattle over the Marlborough Park crossover on Malone Road that featured on the indicator blinds as a short working, 3 November 1951.

Right: On the penultimate day of tram services, No 251 rests at Malone Road terminus, 3 November 1951.

DONEGALL ROAD–LIGONIEL

From the 1930s this seems to have been relatively unaltered; number 35 ran via Shankill Road and 36 via Crumlin Road. The Donegall Road leg of a not inconsiderable journey went over to motor-bus operations on 21 April 1947. After this date Ligoniel cars found other cross-city termini, as will be seen. Donegall Road itself had a football working (Celtic Park) and used a crossover at Rodney Parade, but Belfast Celtic football team left the Irish League as a result of sectarian unpleasantness that outrivalled Glasgow's.

Right: As it leaves Shaftesbury Square for Donegall Road, No 287 negotiates the sharp reverse curves needed to permit cars on that route to use both Dublin Road and Great Victoria Street. As originally planned, curvature was easier but connected only with Great Victoria Street. The date is 17 April 1947.

Below: Looking downhill from Donegall Road terminus on the same date, with a 'Chamberlain' ready to depart. The double track formerly continued to a junction on Falls Road behind the camera.

LIGONIEL, THE CRUMLIN AND THE SHANKILL

One terminus remains to be visited, accessible over two important traffic arteries — the Shankill and Crumlin roads, each climbing to unite for the steepest gradient of all, the mile-and-a-half from Ardoyne to Ligoniel, perhaps the most interesting terminal on the system. The first terminus had been at St Mark's Church, a quarter of a mile up Ligoniel Road from its junction with Crumlin Road. The gradient worsened past St Mark's and this may have worried the Tramways Committee as no cars were as yet fitted with air brakes. None the less, the double track was extended in 1913 almost half a mile to Mill Avenue, a narrow but level street approached by a hump-backed curve off Ligoniel Road that guaranteed a safe lay-by for trams.

Above: Looking towards Ligoniel Road from Mill Avenue on 25 May 1952, with cars Nos 319 and 164. The course of the loop provided for waiting trams can be seen in the foreground. Its removal was probably the result of increased confidence in braking systems, as illustrated in the following pictures.

Above: A gathering of trams on both tracks at Ligoniel — 'Moffett' No 340 on the LRTL tram tour queues up behind two 'Chamberlains' to reverse in Mill Avenue. The destination on No 381 shows that route 57 is now operating between Ligoniel and the former BCDR station. The date is 6 June 1953.

Left: On the right, Ligoniel Road continues to climb as No 406 comes over the hump from Mill Avenue, also with its 'C.Down Rly' reading on the blind. No 340 is next in the queue on 6 June 1953.

Right: An earlier picture shows Nos 327 and 415 inward-bound at the junction from Ardoyne depot (far right) on 31 May 1950. Up to 1946, Crumlin Road trams turned on a crossover just short of the depot points. It was then moved further uphill and both Shankill and Crumlin short-working cars reversed there.

Left: Here is a Shankill Road car reversing on the 1946 crossover at Ardoyne, which is attracting quite a lot of custom. The Shankill cars previously turned back on Woodvale Road, beyond Holy Cross, whose spire can just be seen. The only vehicle not on rails is a horse-drawn cart, 31 May 1950.

Right: Inward-bound on Crumlin Road No 363 approaches the Oldpark junction on 25 April 1951.

Left: Crumlin Road itself ended at Carlisle Circus and the city-bound trams continued by way of Clifton and Donegall streets. No 416 in Clifton Street carries route number 21 for Springfield in November 1945. The grounds are those of the Belfast Charitable Institute. Coming into the frame is one of NIRTB's skull-cracking Bristol Lodekka buses, which took a lot of getting used to. You had to remember where you were sitting.

Right: The busy junction of Donegall Street, Royal Avenue (left) and York Street had a complicated track layout. Pedestrians were in the majority, however, when this view of No 407 turning into Royal Avenue was taken on 4 October 1948. The tall spire in the background belongs to St Patrick's RC Church.

Left: Among a plethora of Belfast tram photos, we can find only one with a 'Crumlin Road' indicator, and here it is on No 346 which is turning into Donegall Square West from Howard Street during a temporary diversion due to a burst water main in Fisherwick Place on 21 October 1952.

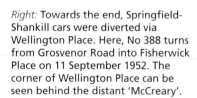

Right: Towards the end, Springfield-Shankill cars were diverted via Wellington Place. Here, No 388 turns from Grosvenor Road into Fisherwick Place on 11 September 1952. The corner of Wellington Place can be seen behind the distant 'McCreary'.

Left: Rebuild No 251 races two bicycles across the Howard Street-Fisherwick Place junction on a Balmoral-Shankill working, 11 September 1952.

Right: Heading for Castle Junction, No 374 rounds the curve at Woodvale Park on 24 October 1952, followed by a lorry (how small they were in those days) and a 'McCreary'. At the kerb is a battery-operated Ormeau bread van.

Left: The bread-server is still busy somewhere as No 406 heads city-ward on Woodvale corner moments later that October afternoon.

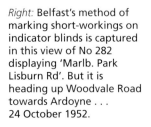

Right: Belfast's method of marking short-workings on indicator blinds is captured in this view of No 282 displaying 'Marlb. Park Lisburn Rd'. But it is heading up Woodvale Road towards Ardoyne . . . 24 October 1952.

AROUND THE CITY CENTRE

Right: In preparation for the change-over to buses on the Balmoral route, it was found necessary to install a crossover in Fisherwick Place as a turning-point for Ligoniel trams. With the Georgian façade of College Square North as a back-scene, No 432 rests in a relatively quiet street dominated by the massive College of Technology in Portland stone on 21 May 1953.

Below: Waiting till that pesky UTA bus is out of the way, No 374's conductor gets ready to place his trolley on the northbound wire in Fisherwick Place. 'City Hall' was chosen as the official destination. A trifle misleading, but who would print new blinds in the last months of Belfast's trams? 31 March 1953.

Right: No 437 is turning into Wellington Place (which has not altogether recovered from wartime austerity), entirely ignored by the 'Black Man' on his plinth. As Mike Maybin has pointed out, the Reverend Cooke's statue is not black, but folk memory of a previous occupant of the plinth has not been eradicated. It is 3 November 1952.

Right: It is the 14th day of September 1945. Belfast is in a celebratory mood. Hostilities had ceased that summer, and a famous Ulsterman, Field Marshal Sir Bernard Montgomery, is being honoured with the freedom of the city. The ceremony, in the City Hall, has necessitated closure of most of Donegall Square to public transport. Here we see car No 284 on a little-used curve from Wellington Place into Donegall Square West. Route 27 (Stranmillis-LMS NCC), among others, has been temporarily severed. Note crowd-barriers in the background.

Left: 'Monty' is being dined (but not wined — he was a total abstainer) in the City Hall. The crossover half-way along Donegall Place-Castle Lane is behind the car — and is seeing unaccustomed use as trams from north and west of the city, including No 428 seen here, are turned back.

Right: Other cars have come into town via Donegall Street and High Street and will leave via Castle Junction and Royal Avenue, like this war-weary red car No 129 heading for the Shankill by a right turn into High Street from Bridge Street. Remains of wartime white paint can be seen on the fender.

BREAKDOWNS AND DERELICTS

Right: On Saturday 22 June 1948 something has happened to 'long top saloon' red car No 182, which has been shunted into the York Street end of Whitla Street and is about to be towed away by its sister No 65. The tram in rear is on the Stranmillis route and will reverse direction without being delayed. In the foreground can be seen the double track that had connected with York Road. By now it has been cut back at the NCC siding (out of sight on left) but overhead wires are still in position.

Left: Confusion on 18 April 1947, outside the Belfast Bank on the Waring Street-Donegall Street S-bend. The disabled 'McCreary' has lost its trolley-head. This had broken an end window in the upper saloon on its way to the ground. The offending hardware seems to have been 'jury-rigged' back into position. A Glengormley car is about to push the streamliner clear of the busy crossing while a policeman peers anxiously around the front of the car. Demolition following the Blitz has revealed the Grand Central Hotel on the skyline. By the end of the century the hotel had become another vanished Belfast landmark.

Right: The Transport Department's permanent way yard was situated on the Madrid Street side of Mountpottinger depot. It was served by a siding that made a sharp left-hand turn from the restricted laneway that gave access to the car shed. As the system shrank, the yard began to be used for tram disposal, though wartime demands curtailed this activity. On 4 September 1945 red cars Nos 36, 181 (long top saloon) and 171 are being broken up.

Above: Saturday shoppers in Castle Place seem unconcerned by the farewell procession of trams heading for Ardoyne depot from Queen's Road, though a respectable (and respectful?) crowd of mourners are lining the tracks at Castle Junction. The Junction had been the busy hub of the system from horse-tram days, so it was a fitting place for a send-off.

Left: The procession of 'Chamberlains' snakes its way through the double junction leading from Crumlin Road to Ardoyne, last operative depot on Belfast Tramways. Note the special double-decker bus waiting to ferry returning VIPs to City Hall, hopefully for something warm on that chilly February day. It was not ideal weather for photography either. For the next several weeks the midnight sounds of tramcars would invade the sleep of those citizens who dwelt alongside the tramlines between Ardoyne and Mountpottinger depot, where the trams were being broken up.